BACKSTAGE PASS

NAOMI STRIEMER

BACKSTAGE PASS
THE NAOMI STRIEMER STORY

Pacific Press®
Publishing Association

Nampa, Idaho | Oshawa, Ontario, Canada
www.pacificpress.com

Cover design by Gerald Lee Monks
Cover resources from the author
Inside design by Kristin Hansen-Mellish
Inside photos provided by the author

The author assumes full responsibility for the accuracy of all facts and quotations as cited in this book.

Additional copies of this book may be obtained by calling toll-free 1-800-765-6955 or online at http://www.aventistbookcenter.com.

Library of Congress Cataloging-in-Publication Data:

Striemer, Naomi, 1982–
  Backstage pass : the Naomi Striemer story / Naomi Striemer.
     p. cm.
  ISBN 13: 978-0-8163-4518-2 (pbk.)
  ISBN 10: 0-8163-4518-X (pbk.)
  1. Striemer, Naomi, 1982– 2. Singers—United States—Biography.
3. Contemporary Christian musicians—United States—Biography. 4. Popular music—Religious aspects—Christianity. I. Title.
  ML420.S9175A3 2013
  782.42164092—dc23
  [B]
                          2013006570

13 14 15 16 17 • 5 4 3 2 1

Dedication

I would like to dedicate this book to my husband, Jordan, who constantly inspires me to push through my doubts and fears to accomplish anything I set my mind to. My parents, Glen and Lorraine, for being an integral part of this journey, without whom this story would never have been possible. Darlene Schacht for getting me started with the first two chapters and teaching me a great deal about book writing. And, most important, my Lord and Savior Jesus, for loving me, dying for me, and never forsaking me.

Contents

Chapter 1   The Big Deal   9
Chapter 2   Mud Boots and Milking Goats   21
Chapter 3   First Recordings   27
Chapter 4   Chasing the Dream   39
Chapter 5   Entertaining the World   53
Chapter 6   911   69
Chapter 7   Six Months of Mourning   81
Chapter 8   Touring the Next Chapter   91
Chapter 9   Safe-House   95
Chapter 10   Hollywood Walk of Fame   103
Chapter 11   At the Crossroads   119
Chapter 12   America's Idol   125
Chapter 13   My Incomparable God   137
Photo Gallery   143

Chapter 1
The Big Deal

"Can you sing one of your songs to me—live?" he asked.

Nervous, yet trying my best to appear calm, I stood up, opened my mouth and began to sing "Are You OK?" This was something I had never experienced before—having to sing for a crowd of one, and not just an audience of one, but potentially the single most important person of my career up to that point.

I tried to imagine where a professional might focus her gaze. *Where am I supposed to look? Into his eyes? Over his head? Or beyond the glass of the window that separated us from the world?* Unsure of myself, I chose all three, every now and then catching a glimpse of what might be his smile. Not wanting to reveal the truth in my eyes—that this confident, self-assured, eighteen-year-old girl was pretending to be everything she wanted to be until someone would validate what she truly was, and what she always had dreamed she would be.

While the rest of New York City was bustling below, we were sitting in a corner office on the twenty-second floor of the Sony Tower. Although windows consumed much of the space, one couldn't help but notice the walls covered in platinum records, and the shelves filled with awards from artists I had admired over the years. It was *surreal.*

I also noticed the two or three small piles of CDs on his desk. They were demo CDs sent in by artists who, after what were most certainly agonizing months of preparation, blood, sweat, and tears, hoped to have a chance to be in the very spot I was in at that moment. Ninety-nine percent of those artists would never sit in this office. Instead, they would receive a polite, "Not interested at this time" letter in the mail. Those few were the very last ones that had made it through the hundreds sent in each week, screened by trained staff before landing on the vice president's desk. And here I was face-to-face in his office.

I had envisioned this moment a thousand times in my imagination, but not one of those dreams had prepared me for the dry throat, sweaty hands, and overwhelming sense of intimidation I felt. I was uneasy, but wouldn't let fear come between me and my dream. This was the shot I had waited for my entire life, and I wasn't about to let it pass by.

Once I finished the song, Dave excused himself from the room. In fact, he had left the room several times during our interview, leaving me to wonder if I had messed up somehow. My only conclusion was that he was either bored stiff—or incredibly rude. Either way, there was something far more interesting on the other side of the wall that called his attention time and again.

During those two hours, he asked all sorts of questions about my personal life and my dreams for the future. He asked me to sing a second song, and then the first one again, until finally he said, "I can't pretend any longer. I have been back and forth on the phone with the president of the label."

I could feel my heart's wild thumping at each beat.

"She is at a showcase right now," he said, leaning over his desk, "but I've been urging her to leave the showcase to come back here and meet you. That's why I've been trying to hold you here for so long."

The room fell silent for a second or two as I took in every word that he said. My mom was sitting next to me, and although I wasn't facing her, I felt her excitement surrounding us.

"There is nothing more I can do today," Dave concluded. "Will you be here tomorrow?"

There was a problem with saying Yes. One was that my mom and I had a return flight home booked for the next day, and, second, my parents couldn't afford this trip, never mind paying for additional ac- commodations and flight-change fees that staying an extra day would surely incur.

"I can be," I said, "but my flight and hotel would have to be changed. I am scheduled to fly out in the morning."

I later came to realize that money wasn't an issue when it came to Sony Records. But at that point in life, my family was driving on fumes and pinching the few pennies we had just spent on my career. There was no more money coming down the pipe.

"Give me your travel details," he said, rising from his chair, "and we'll reschedule it for you. You can see my assistant outside my office, and she'll give you information on a new hotel this evening, and flight details. A car will be waiting for you downstairs, and the driver will take you to your current hotel to gather your things and relocate you to the new hotel."

And just like that, arrangements were made. I was instructed to relax for the evening and wait for a call in the morning, at which time they would set up an appointment between me, Dave, and the president of Sony Records.

My heart's desire

After shaking hands with Dave, my mother and I walked out of that building on Madison Avenue, and I took my first step into a new life that was unfolding before me. It was a chilly afternoon in February; the sun had already set, but I was warm beneath the sense of exhilaration and the beige fur coat that my mom and I had picked out from a secondhand store the week before.

"If you want to be a star," she told me, "you have to dress like one." And so my mom and dad sacrificed their own wants and desires to nurture my dreams in every way that they could. Mom had become my stylist, my hairdresser, and my assistant while my father had shared the position of my spiritual advisor, my mentor, and my best friend along with her.

My parents had decided long before that they could sit at home, on a farm in the middle of nowhere, and grow old; or they could invest their time and money in my future. And so they gave of themselves time and again, nurturing me physically, mentally, and spiritually in the best way they knew how.

I know that I owe a lot to my father's deeply grounded spiritual roots and my mother's creative, joyful, and inquisitive mind. The ideas and questions they posed every day offered me a balance between the two that I grew into. I was a daughter of missionary parents who had decided she was going to pursue a lifestyle and career in mainstream pop music—a career choice that most Christian parents warned their children to stay away from; a place that was full of "sin, drugs, and rock-and-roll."

While I had a desire to sing mainstream music, I also had a strong desire to serve God and share His Word. This is who I was, and I had a plan. Deep down in my heart, I believed God and my parents would appreciate my plan, even though I had done more telling than asking or listening when it came down to the details.

Why mainstream? That was a question I had been asked, and seemed like I had been answering for years.

The first thing that came to mind was Céline Dion. It was her voice—that magnificent, controlled, and powerful voice—that drew me with jaw-dropping awe to the industry. But that was only the tip of a large iceberg that filled the answer to that question. I thought I had my future mapped out, and for the time being, God was letting me lead in the direction I wanted to take.

Wonderland

The lobby was a stark contrast to the shabby old hotel we had just left with aged mirrors on each wall that gave the illusion it was much larger than it actually was. This hotel resembled an abstract art festival with a hint of Wonderland woven throughout, and every guest was playing Alice. It had a peculiar edgy yet breathtaking décor with unusual chairs and sofas of all sorts scattered around the large, dimly lit lobby filled with carefully placed tiny white candles.

Some chairs were enormous and made you look small, while some were tiny and made you look big. Some others were skinny, and some were wide. We saw chairs carved out of exotic tree trunks, and metal ones with twisting, turning branches rising from the back; others were fashioned in prints and buttons you'd never imagine seeing alone, let alone together. A gigantic vase filled with flowering branches illuminated by changing colored lights stood near the elevators. It appeared far too beautiful to be real, but it was. The flowers seemed to symbolize natural beauty as people utterly consumed with their lives passed it too quickly to grasp its significance.

This hotel was unlike anything we had seen before, and it was our lodging for the night.

The next morning, my mom and I made our way down to the hotel restaurant to grab something to eat. I would have been fine staying in the white hotel room to study the painting that formed the headboard of my bed and relive each moment as it was happening. But Mom insisted on breakfast because everything was being paid for, including the nine-dollar macadamia nuts from the mini bar I had chastised her for eating the night before.

But the truth is that food was the last thing on my mind. I had to mentally prepare; I couldn't start to relax now, not after so much work to get to this point. In addition, I didn't want Sony to think I was taking advantage of them by racking up a big bill. Little did I know the only person who would ever see this bill would be an assistant who would care very little about two breakfasts and a few nuts.

It was 9:38 A.M. I know that because I remember looking at my watch every two minutes or so. The smell of fresh Belgian waffles hung in the air—Mom's, not mine. I had opted for oatmeal and fruit. I couldn't forsake my routine on the most important day of my life. I wasn't sure that even oatmeal would set well—not with the anticipation and anxiety I was feeling. My mother was leisurely sipping her orange juice and taking some vitamins while I shifted in my chair, trying to send a message that we had no time to waste; that we really needed to get back upstairs.

All I could think of was the phone call we had been told to expect. What time would the meeting be? What if I only had a short time to get ready? And what if they were trying to call while we were sitting downstairs? Mr. Dave Massey had told me they would be in touch the next morning, but time was slipping away—and I had a million things to go through before I would be mentally prepared. I had to envision the meeting and every answer to every question they might ask; I had to create a map for my voice to present the song in just the right way: the melody I would pull the most feeling from, the notes and words I would deliver with the most power, the tender sections where I would allow my voice to crack ever so slightly. And again, where would I look? I had to know in advance this time. My mother had said that eye contact is most important, but I couldn't stand the intimacy of such a delivery. And what if the president asked me to sing a different song? Or didn't ask me to sing one at all?

This is it

Thoughts became a reality the moment we got back to the room. There was a phone call from Sony—I had a 1:00 P.M. meeting with them.

This had to be it, I thought. *I'm going to get my record deal today.* Every muscle in my body was tense and held their grip on me until later that evening. There was no room for error. I had to be exactly what they were looking for.

My courage and grit convinced me I was, and I wouldn't let one moment of doubt constrict me. There simply wasn't another option after all that I had put my family through to get here. I had been preparing for this day, for this moment, constantly for four intense years. This was Epic Records we were talking about. They represented The Jacksons, ABBA, Céline Dion, Aerosmith, Jennifer Lopez, Mariah Carey, Barbara Streisand—and could it be Naomi Striemer? They were looking for the next major recording star, and I had to prove I was "it."

We returned to the lobby at 550 Madison Avenue, where I reported to the nearest reception desk on the second floor. The building was extraordinary with its thirty-foot interior walls and twenty-foot paintings, but not quite as impressive as the artists within. It was commonplace to see a familiar face or two walking by. In fact that very morning we saw three: Patrick Monahan, Jimmy Stafford, and Scott Underwood from Train were checking in just a few feet away. I would come to learn over time that no one stepped onto those elevators without first checking in for meeting confirmation, a name, and photo pass—regardless of how big a star you might be.

Meeting the president

Stepping off of the elevator on the twenty-third floor, my mom and I were greeted by an assistant who led us down a long hallway passing dozens of cubicles and open doors along the way. We were directed to Polly Anthony's office, and judging from the size of her office, it may have spanned the entire width of that floor. It was beautifully designed with a slight feminine touch.

While I was hoping for a warm reception from the president of Epic Records, I was met with a no-nonsense, friendly but firm invitation. "Take a seat," she said.

There were three seating choices—the back wall, where my mom chose to stay, the middle area, where the vice president sat, and another two chairs close to her desk. I approached her alone and took one of those chairs.

After barking at her assistant about a lunch order filled incorrectly, she flashed me the customary smile and leaned back in her chair. "Sing me the song you sang to Dave yesterday."

Meanwhile, a salad was placed on her desk—a peace offering for the lunch they messed up. "Hold on." She stopped me before I could begin. Grabbing her salad, she took a seat in the middle section beside Mr. Massey.

Standing, I turned to face them both. I sang like I had the day before, but this time the backing music was turned down so low I could barely hear it at all. It was awkward enough singing to a stone-faced woman with unblinking eye contact, without a glitch in the music potentially throwing me off.

I had to present myself the best way I could. So I stopped and asked if the music could be turned a little louder.

"No, I intended for it to be this low," she said, resting her fork in her salad.

I started in once again, determined to deliver the greatest performance of my life. There was no giving up.

An orange dot on the wall

The moment I finished the song, a smile crossed her face, followed by a round of applause and some clarification, "I turned down the music because I wanted to make sure that there weren't any tricks involved," she said. "I wanted to ensure that what I was hearing was your voice—nothing else."

My head was reeling from her response. I was sitting with the president of Epic Records, and from what I could tell, she was pleased with my voice. I had never before felt exhilaration like this. I was numb with joy, but what did her response mean? What—if anything—was next? Questions, hopes, and fear were all getting ahead of me. I had to stop my racing thoughts in order to listen.

"How do you envision yourself as an artist?" Polly asked.

"Well," I smiled, sitting at the edge of my chair, "if all of the music out there is gray, I want to be the orange dot on the wall. I want to stand out and be different."

I was pretty happy with what I considered a clever answer, but apparently she wasn't. "Honey," she said, "considering we produce most of that 'gray' music out there, why don't you aim for a darker or different shade of gray? Try to be *that* different—and you won't fit into any radio station that I know of."

Not such a great answer when she put it that way. While I was trying to figure out how to recover from that blunder, she managed to segue in a better direction.

Joining the family

I don't remember much of what was said after that, if we talked about family, any current obligations, or what other labels I had met with on my trip. I just remember what she said thirty-five minutes into our conversation. "How would you like to join the Sony family?" she asked, leaning in.

I wasn't sure how to answer that because I wasn't sure what she meant. I remember thinking, *Did she just ask me if I wanted to join Sony? She hadn't asked if I wanted to produce a record. Is this a hypothetical question, or was an offer just thrown on the table?*

I had prepared to do my best, but was unprepared to handle the very question that could change my life as I knew it.

Searching for words, I replied, "I would absolutely love that!"

Based on her experience, she knew just what to say next, "I think it's time we give your attorney Peter Lewit a call to tell him the good news!" And while she dialed the phone number, I struggled to process what was happening there.

Peter Lewit was my prominent-yet-hip New York lawyer. He looked like a rock star with salt-and-pepper hair to his shoulders, and he knew how to handle all things relating to the industry—including an offer from Sony.

Peter recognized the number on his caller ID. "How is it going?" his voice chimed through the speaker.

"Well, we think she's great, Peter. We want to sign your girl!"

"Congratulations, Naomi, you've done a great job!" His voice was calm yet confident, and I sensed the satisfaction in his tone. He and Polly talked for only a few more minutes as Peter said it had been a long day and suggested they begin discussions tomorrow.

Rising from our chairs, we shook hands, concluded the meeting, and walked out of Polly's office. We didn't make it twenty feet down the hallway before the phones started to ring. Peter was calling my cell phone to congratulate me again, while I was notified of another call on line two.

"Hello?" I said, wondering who could possibly know I was there. It was Jim Welch, my original contact from my first meeting at Sony Records—the man who had called me on Friday evening, hours after initially meeting, to ask if I could come back in to Sony to meet with Dave Massey for a meeting on Monday. It was now Tuesday. This man would later become my AR (artist and repertoire) within the label. Basically, he became my go-to person at Sony, handling everything music-related for me.

Jim was congratulating me, while simultaneously admitting some confusion. "Everyone is holding their breath," he said, "and Polly is wondering if you might play us against other labels."

What I had intended to be an absolute, positive, undeniable "Yes," Polly had understood as a "Maybe." There was nothing I wanted more than to sign with Epic Records, and the opportunity had finally arrived.

The world stopped turning for a moment as all things moved in slow motion. Employees were hugging me, shaking my hand, patting my back, and telling me how much they were looking forward to working with me.

God's incomparable grace

This is what success feels like, I thought, as I heard my mom excitedly chatting with some of the staffers before I felt her arm slip around my shoulders and pull me in for a hug.

A car was waiting downstairs to take us to the airport, but before leaving New York, my mom had a stop to make at the florist. It was Valentine's Day, and the person who had been with me through every up and down I'd faced in my life returned to the car with a bouquet of roses for me.

Picking up the cell phone, I dialed home. "Dad," I said, "I got the deal at Sony." And together we praised God for His incomparable grace.

When departing on this trip, I had promised my dad I wasn't leaving New York City without a record deal. Everyone I knew in the business said it was impossible and couldn't be done in a week. But here I was, having achieved that one-in-a-million possibility.

I was loved by a God who had not only given me the gift of song, but also my lifelong dream of working with Sony Records. I hadn't taken the time to ask God if this was what He saw for my life. Since the age of thirteen, I had determined to be a good role model and to be an influence that was lacking in mainstream music. I had received offers from Christian labels when I was younger, but with a conscious decision to go into mainstream, I believed I could reach the unreached. I would simply keep my career and beliefs separate.

I had pursued my dream. I had a plan. I had a list of things that I wanted to do. And without considering the desire of my Savior's heart, I followed my own.

View from the top

The next two months were a time of planning and learning. I had a contract as thick as a phone book to go through. In addition to my lawyer, I needed to secure a money manager—and basically had my choice when it came to managers.

Things started to move quickly. Upon signing the deal, one hundred thousand dollars was deposited into my bank account, with their commitment to spend a minimum of seven hundred fifty thousand on the record.

I was put on a seven-hour flight to London, where I'd be working with the top producers in the world. Able to bring one person with me, I chose my mom to come along on the trip. Like two schoolgirls, we giggled and prattled and played with the items the airline supplied for our flight. There's something funny about eye covers, blankets, and "Virgin" socks when you're overtired and excited beyond words.

Thirty-seven thousand feet above the earth we fell asleep, happy that I had finally made it and excited by what lay ahead. I had a view from the top of the world—standing on the peak of a mountain that was about to come crumbling down.

Chapter 2
Mud Boots and Milking Goats

Taking in my first breath, I came into this world on October 6, 1982. And they called me Naomi, a Hebrew name meaning "beautiful, pleasant, delightful." No words could possibly describe my childhood any better than that except one might add *unusual*.

The events surrounding my birth are somewhat peculiar, but to Glen and Lorraine Striemer, this was everyday life as they knew it to be.

After much study and deliberation, my parents decided it was in my best interest to be delivered at home: quiet, calm, intimate, and most important—natural. Not our home actually, but an old house deep in the countryside. And so they journeyed with my brother, Nathan, to Upstate New York, where they stayed in the home of renowned midwife Louise Dull until the time of my arrival.

It was early evening when she heard the racket. A group of horses from a neighboring farm had gotten out of their paddock where a gate came undone and were running loose on the road. Being the high-spirited and fearless woman she is, my mom pursued them without hesitation, and amid all this excitement, she went into labor.

With the onset of painful contractions and broken water signifying that my time had come, she made her way back to the house to give birth to her child.

Mount Missionary

Not long before I was born, my parents left everything behind to join a small community on a mountaintop in New Hampshire known as "Mount Missionary." It was there that they were trained to share the gospel and absorb an entirely new way of living based on simplicity, health, and a deep dedication to God. They were basically hippies going the opposite way of vegetarian farming, who put on the brakes and turned their lives completely around, adopting a healthy lifestyle and profound faith in Christ. So strong were their convictions that they eliminated foods such as caffeine and white sugar, while adding herbs and berries and seeds.

Gone were the days of managing rock bands and selling ads for a Toronto entertainment magazine. Leaving all that behind them, they were content to survive on little to nothing, and to endure hardships and conditions that came their way. They learned to grow things, to barter, and to survive off the land.

My introduction to music

As morning broke, some of the ladies came down from the mountain to visit us at the house. They were as eager to see the new baby as we were to see them. Nestled within the warmth of my mother's arms, I peered over the flannel of my white blanket, barely able to open my eyes, too young to understand, yet old enough to know I was loved. Serenaded with scripture-laced lyrics of "The King's Daughter," "Naomi," and other songs they composed, I drifted to sleep with the ebb and flow of the melody. This set the tone to a lifelong symphony of music.

My arrival put a wrench in Mommy and Dad's plans of going to Africa. Because they had a new baby girl, it was decided that the best place to send this missionary family was to Nova Scotia, where my dad would sell Bibles and related products in the Maritime Provinces. And so when I was two years old, we made the move.

Humble home in Nova Scotia

Packing everything we had into our old van, my parents, Nathan, and I left our home on Mount Missionary to start a new life on a small farm in Nova Scotia.

For only one hundred dollars a month, my parents rented a dilapidated old farm house nine miles from the main road. It was on a point surrounded by ocean on three sides, and that might have been breathtaking had the house not been in dire need of repair. My mom was optimistic about transforming that house into a home. And she did. My mom was a powerhouse when it came to rolling up her sleeves and getting to work.

Dad picked up a small yellow Toyota that we referred to as "the lemon." Monday to Friday the lemon was gone, and Dad along with it. He would sleep in the car or find church people to stay with, but for the rest of the time he was on the road selling Bibles and Christian resources.

My mom was at home, looking after my brother and me and taking care of the house. There was a lot of work for her to do, taking care of a toddler, homeschooling Nathan, feeding the animals, tending to the gardens, and fixing up the house—but as we grew, so did our list of chores. Some of which I liked—others not so much.

We had a one-acre garden that we had to weed and care for all summer. My brother hated it, but I didn't mind. In fact, half of the time I'd pretend I was weeding, while I was eating peas and tomatoes out in the garden.

Eventually Mom was homeschooling the both of us, and part of that schooling included learning how to live off the land and the importance of animal husbandry.

Unlike other children, we didn't know what pop and chips were, so on the rare occasion that we'd have guests over, we'd feast on lettuce and beans with their kids. That's all we knew, and when you become so accustomed to eating this way, it's all you want.

My love for life

Because of our love for living things, we acquired animals of every kind, but unlike other farmers, we didn't eat our pets—yes, even the cows were my "pets." In fact, I remember one Sunday when a farmer came by to pick up a few of our chickens, he made a remark that horrified us. "That chicken will look great on my plate!" he said. "I'll just lop his head off and we're good to go."

Plate? Lop his head off? This was Clucky we were talking about, a pet I had cared for since she was a chick. As far as we were concerned, chickens supplied our eggs, goats and cows gave us milk, and sheep gave us wool. But most important, they gave us companionship, and that was the lesson my parents instilled in us from the day that we got our first cow.

There was a rule in our house: we didn't eat until the animals were all fed, so chores were done first thing every morning.

As I got older, I was put in charge of milking the goats, which I like to think I was good at. Should I forget to bring the milk in or turn my back on the bucket, the kittens would be in there wetting their whiskers, but I was careful to make sure that didn't happen often. I would bring the white bucket of fresh milk into the house, where my mother would strain it while it was still warm.

Beautiful, breathtaking, unusual life

In addition to doing our schoolwork, we'd study the Scriptures and play. I understood that the Bible was the "living" Word, and I was convinced that I'd have my chance to be written into it too. Nathan and I would run around the farm with towels on our heads playing that we were two of the biblical children of Israel. And then we'd grab our towels and head down to the beach, where we'd spend hours making sand castles and burying our feet deep in the sand.

From the crack of dawn to the setting of the sun, I spent most of my days outside. Without television or alternative forms of media, Nathan and I found plenty of things to do. We'd run through the fields playing hide-and-go-seek, and we'd ride our dirt bikes down the various trails leading to the beach and back home again. We took our small rowboat onto the tiny pond a few hundred feet from the house, and we built tree forts and villages in the woods.

Many evenings were spent playing board games, but nothing compared to the beauty of the tranquil evenings I spent in the barn, listening to the animals chewing their hay and drinking their water. It was almost hypnotic to lie there and listen while the kittens pounced and played without care to the rhythm of life. While other children were watching TV, I was curled up in the warmth of a haystack watching a horse giving birth. And while other kids were spending money on CDs and boom boxes, I spent time learning to play the music I loved.

The heartbeat of our home

Music was the heartbeat that set the tempo in our home. Nathan played the piano, but not without a struggle. I always sat to his left, imitating the movement of his hands, until eventually I took over the keys, and the piano seat was my own. Friday evenings Dad would return from his work on the road, and after the dinner dishes were all put away, he'd pull out his guitar for a time of singing and worship. The weekends were also exciting because I knew that we'd be heading off to church, where I'd have another opportunity to sing. We sang so much back in those days, but traditional hymns and songs of Scripture were all that I knew.

I'll never forget the first time I took the stage. I was five years old. My cousin Colleen and I stood in front of an audience of perhaps twenty people, to sing a duet. I sang the first verse, we shared the chorus, and I waited for her to sing the second verse. When nothing happened, I did what any aspiring young artist would do and improvised by singing her lines.

From that moment on, I owned the stage. And every time that my parents sang a duet, it had to be a trio with Naomi standing between them. Barely visible to those in the third row and beyond, this little blond girl stood on tippy toes, finding the notes to sing harmony.

Little did I know that there was a whole other world of music out there. Growing in peace and tranquility, I was sheltered and safe from the world and beyond.

Dr. Betty Murray

We met Dr. Betty Murray one cold December night at a Christmas concert in the small town of Tatamagouche. In a beautiful old-fashioned church, the choir sang Handel's *Messiah*. I was mesmerized by the beauty of it all. The music, the lyrics, and the presentation were all impeccably timed down to the last detail. It was no surprise that visitors from the big city would come to this concert every year saying that this was the best choir they'd heard. We had to be a part of this beauty.

From that day on, we met Dr. Murray and her group in a school gymnasium each Monday evening. Sitting in a semicircle, we rehearsed and we trained under the direction of a stern yet talented doctor of music.

"Stop! Stop! Stop!" she'd command. "Judith, you're singing flat. You need to lift your voice! John, you're mumbling your words!" She'd holler, "You need to enunciate. If spit isn't flying out of your mouth, you're not clear enough!"

And while Dr. Murray directed the choir, she tapped and tapped and tapped the rhythm of each song out on my leg, so that it was pink by the end of the evening. It has often been said that she engrained rhythm into my body those Monday evenings.

Our choir sang at various community events, and sometimes we'd assemble with other choirs as well. But the big event came each July, when we'd perform weeklong plays at the local hockey arena. Adding to the excitement of being on stage was hearing that Dr. Murray's niece was in the audience. Anne Murray was a Canadian superstar and Grammy Award winner who would often come to watch us perform.

Dr. Murray began hosting an extra event in her beautiful, historic home. Saturday evenings we'd sit in her sun room singing and talking and sharing stories about her family history. One Saturday evening after the rest of the guests had left, she turned to my parents to say, "Naomi has a very special voice. She has the potential to be a Barbara Streisand–type girl."

I had no idea who Barbara Streisand was. In fact, I didn't even know what a radio was until I happened upon one at nine years old. But once that radio came on, I was sold. I was a singer, and this is what I wanted to do with the rest of my life.

Chapter 3
First Recordings

I was nine years old. I remember waiting for my parents outside of church after the service. It was an early summer day, and a teenage girl I didn't know very well started talking to me. We walked toward her parents' car, she opened the door, sat down, and asked what singers I liked. She kept saying names, and I kept shaking my head No. She turned a few dials on this thing she called "the radio," and suddenly music started to play. She shrieked with joy—her favorite song was playing!

It was the first time I'd ever heard the radio.

A lot of things were about to change in my life, and hearing the radio was just the beginning. My peaceful, wholesome, simple life was coming to an end.

Leaving the farm

I stood at the end of the hallway gazing out the window down at my parents who were having a heated conversation. My mother's hands flew into the air as she turned toward the barn. A trailer pulled into the yard; animals started to be brought out and loaded in. One by one, day after day, they left: sheep, goats, cows, chickens, ducks, and finally … the horses.

I'll never forget the look on my mom's face as that last trailer filled with the very animals she had rescued, and some that she had raised from birth, were taken away.

We were moving. Moving from the only home I had ever known. Life would never again be the same.

Our new home in Manitoba was small, surrounded by fields. It was here, in this tiny rural community, that I would begin to sing in churches. I desperately missed the Monday night choir practice, the

Christmas concerts, and most of all, the plays. In order to fill this void, I began to beg my dad for singing opportunities in the bigger surrounding cities.

One thing lead to another, discovering television lead to cable, choosing radio in the car over playing tapes, country music lead to pop music, watching movies for the first time, celebrating my tenth and eleventh birthdays, and then finding myself headed to a recording studio.

Excitement filled my heart, thoughts of joy and my future as a singer filled my mind! And then it all came crashing to a halt as we pulled up to a small bungalow house, with five feet of plowed snow on each side of the driveway. I thought, *Where is the recording studio?*

Then my father was saying, "Here we are! Let's go."

"I'm not going in there," I declared. "That's not a studio!"

"Naomi, don't be like that. These are very nice people; they're expecting us, now come on."

He opened his door and got out. I stayed firmly planted in my seat.

I was a shy girl to most, but at eleven and twelve, I had already developed a mind of my own, one that had high expectations. A makeshift little home recording studio wasn't what I considered a "real" recording studio. *How embarrassing to go into some stranger's house to sing songs,* I thought. It just seemed awkward and humiliating. Little did I know I would later record in closets, bathrooms, living rooms, and hallways to further my career.

After I sat alone in the minivan for ten minutes pondering my decision, I was ready to give it a shot. Right then my father reappeared at the door. We walked together across the street and into the little house.

Four hours later, we emerged with a proud tape of my recordings in hand. Eight songs and two piano pieces, which I had composed on the spot. I barely remembered my hesitation at this point. I was excited looking ahead into my future.

Public school

I made the decision to go to public school, as opposed to Christian or private school, when I was twelve because I wanted to try it out. My parents didn't oppose my choice because it meant I would stay close to home. My brother had gone to a private Christian school, but that meant he lived with a family a few hours away, or in a dormitory, depending on which year of school he was in.

By the time I was in tenth grade, I had one thing on my mind and one thing only: the Backstreet Boys. The boy band had just released their first album, and I remember falling in love instantly: the music, the words, their dance moves, and those faces! I picked a favorite member pretty quickly, obviously the one closest to me in age with the blond hair and blue eyes; I would sit for hours listening and singing along to their music.

It wasn't long before I had read and memorized every word in the CD booklet and began to look at every songwriter, producer, recording studio, manager, label, and even manufacturer.

The wheels in my mind were turning. Obviously, I was going to become a famous female pop singer, and the Backstreet Boys and I would tour around the world together. My favorite member and I would date, and I could kiss cold Canada, the prairies, and small towns goodbye and live the life I was destined for, superstardom, forever! Or so I thought.

I began having vivid dreams of being backstage at big concerts, conversations I would have with these pop stars, and studios I would record in.

My worst nightmare was that I would be locked in the life that surrounded me. All these people who had grown up, married, lived, and died in the same place, doing the same things day in and day out. Never having big dreams or getting out.

I felt that I was made for something more. I was special and I didn't fit in with all of the other kids my age; our goals and interests were different. As I saw it, I just had to find a way to get to the right people and make them see it as well.

A new home

My parents had purchased a piece of land forty-five minutes away from the nearest town. It had a barn, a few old sheds, dozens of oak trees, a few ponds, and one really old house. They spent a year renovating the old house before we moved in: new flooring, carpets, kitchen, bathrooms—everything. There wasn't a hint of what used to be there once they were finished. The only thing missing were two bedroom doors—mine and my brothers.

Privacy sheets went up and when my CD player would start blasting Céline Dion, Whitney, and Mariah—and oh yes, plenty of Backstreet—my brother would let it be known he was not thrilled.

"Turn that down!" he would yell. "Mom, can you tell her to *shut up!*"

Being at an age where I really looked up to my brother, I'd quickly grab the knob and turn it down feeling embarrassed he'd heard me singing along. Sometimes I'd retaliate with a classic, "It's not that loud!"

But I knew if I was going to enjoy my music, I had to find another place to play it.

My dad made an office in one of the heavily insulated old sheds near the house. It was narrow and long, and both walls were stacked with boxes of books. It was isolated enough that nobody in the house would hear anything going on in there. I'd found my spot!

When my dad was in the yard working or out selling books, it was perfect. I would bring my CD player, set it on one of the boxes, play my favorite songs as loud as I liked, and sing along. My favorite CD to do this with was Céline Dion's. I loved her voice—she sang so perfectly. If only I could one day sing as well as she did.

Then it hit me, I could keep up with most of the singers on most of the songs. Maybe it wasn't an impossible dream after all; an exuberant thought rushed into my head: *I can actually do this!*

Technology comes to the farm

There it sat, our first computer, bulky and large on a desk upstairs. My gateway to the world outside! Chat rooms, e-mail addresses, and hours spent waiting for Web sites to load on dial-up Internet. It didn't take long before I was bringing those CD booklets to the desk, setting them next to the keyboard, and typing into the search engine the names I found: songwriters, producers, studios, and labels.

I had hit the jackpot! One of the producers mentioned several times on many albums had a studio! It had an address! And it was in Sweden.

I quickly jotted the information down on a piece of paper, ran downstairs and out the front door to my dad, who was cutting wood in front of his office. Without a moment to catch my breath, I excitedly exclaimed. "Dad, I have to go to Sweden!"

Puzzled, he looked up from the pile of wood.

"One of the biggest producers in the world who does everything has a studio there, and I have the address. I know if I go I could become a pop star!" I said, waving the piece of paper around before he could ask any questions.

"You're not going to Sweden," Dad said matter-of-factly.

I was shocked, heartbroken. How could he destroy my amazing discovery like that without even a discussion? I went back inside the house disappointed, sat back down at the computer, and thought, *There's a way; I just have to find it.*

Career versus school: The negotiation

I began gaining a social life, throwing parties because I wasn't allowed to go to any, skipping classes because I couldn't hang out with anyone after school because of my direct ride in and out with a neighbor each day. So I made time during math to indulge in social activities, spending time in a dingy smoke-filled basement with one of my brother's friends, who had been expelled from school.

I knew I had been found out when the phone rang and it was handed to me; it was my mom asking why I wasn't in class. My geography teacher had ratted me out, calling to alert my mother of the situation. It was actually a good thing because a few more skipped classes and I would have not known how to figure simple math or had a chance to learn about all of the countries I would be visiting in the very short years to come.

A few days later my father approached with a compromise; but let's be honest, it was more of a negotiation. He proposed that if I were to go back to homeschooling, he would devote time to my career and act as my music manager. I listened carefully to every word, and after he was finished, I counteroffered. Being a salesman's daughter, I believed there should be terms.

Term 1: I would allow him to manage my music career.

Term 2: I would quit public school only if he devoted enough time to my career.

Term 3: If he did not spend enough time furthering my career, I would return to attending public school.

Let the trial period begin!

First act of business

My father made an appointment at the biggest studio in the province; it was finally time for me to take that next step and see how record making was professionally done.

Anxious and excited, I took the day off school, and we drove the two hours into the big city. My mother came with us and dropped us off in the studio parking lot so she could go to the mall while I recorded.

The building looked like a studio. Finally! A real one. We walked through the double doors into a large foyer with a receptionist, couches, and records on the walls.

I had a song in hand that a singer/songwriter friend of my parents had written. It was the song I'd brought to record that day.

Moments later we were greeted by a clean-cut, sharp looking man who was the owner of the studio and the producer my dad had booked for our session. He led us down the hall to Studio A—the largest room in the building. The studio was lined with wood—the floor, the walls, the counters that held the biggest console filled with knobs that I'd ever seen. A huge glass window divided the room, and behind the glass was a microphone in a room big enough to record an entire orchestra.

We sat down on a black leather couch at the back of the room. The producer sat on his swivel chair and asked what I wanted to accomplish.

I handed him my CD and said, "I'd like to record this song."

Without a word he put the CD into his player, and seconds later all of the speakers surrounding the room were filled with the sound. Twenty seconds went by; then he abruptly leaned over and pressed STOP.

"Do you have anything else?" he asked.

My father and I looked at each other bewildered and confused. "No, just that one song," I replied.

"Do you write your own songs? Maybe we can write something," he said, handing me the CD.

"No, I don't write songs," I paused. "I would like to record that one."

"The song you just gave me isn't going anywhere: it has no hook, the verses are too long, and I'm not going to waste my time recording garbage. You should start writing, kid."

And with that I was infuriated! Who did this man think he was? We had hired *him;* it was our decision what we did with our time. Start writing songs? Please, I would never write songs. My favorite singers never wrote songs.

"Céline Dion doesn't write songs," I retorted.

"Well, you ain't no Céline Dion, kid."

He launched into a story about an artist he had worked with for eleven years perfecting her craft, working on improving her songwriting, and how she had just been signed with Sony Canada. Her name was Chantal Kreviazuk.

All I could hear in that story was "eleven years." It was not going to take me that long; this man had rocks in his head. I would never write songs, and it would never take me *that* long to sign a deal.

We were at an impasse and before wasting any more time, he was ushering us out of Studio A and back into the lobby, telling the receptionist to refund us our money and wishing us luck on our journey.

We stood there, mouths opened, stunned. *What had just happened? Could he do that?* The answer, obviously, was Yes, he could.

My dad, trying to lighten the mood, looked at me and said jokingly, "I've been kicked out of better places than this."

The real question was What were we supposed to do now?

My mother had left us for the afternoon and wasn't scheduled to come back for at least two and a half hours. There was no way of contacting her. We just had to wait. But where would we wait? We couldn't stay there wallowing in our humiliation.

It was minus 30°C but we started walking. It was a rough part of town, but at the end of the block we found a restaurant, which also doubled as a Laundromat. For the next two hours, we talked and laughed as we ate our salad and fries. It may have been a failed attempt at recording, but at least my dad had gotten me out of school.

Songwriting 101

"You're never going to make it unless you start writing songs." Those words kept ringing in my ears. He was wrong. I was going to make it—and songwriting would have nothing to do with it. But just to prove him wrong, maybe I would write a song, just to say I could! Not because I would ever need it.

I pulled out several pieces of paper, grabbed a pencil, and settled on the floor in front of my stereo. I looked through a few CD booklets, glancing at lyrics as I turned the pages. I could do this; it would be easy. I turned on some music low in the background and began to write. The words flowed. And before I knew it, I had dozens of pages surrounding me with stories.

Over the next few weeks, I perfected several of the stories, putting them into verses, a chorus, and a bridge. Then I had to ask myself, What about the music?

I had been playing the piano and writing original melodies on the piano for several years—but the thought never crossed my mind to connect the two. The music in my fingers had remained dormant, disconnected from the songwriter for several years until just the time when I needed it.

My father, in the meantime, had been just as determined as I was to prove that man wrong and not be shut out from the studio permanently. He had begun speaking with the producer in Studio B and had arranged a two-day session to write songs and record.

Three of us entered the studio this time; nobody would be left behind in case things went south. The studio was smaller, less grand, and less wood; but the atmosphere was warm and inviting. The producer in Studio B was definitely a musician: a wool sweater and unkempt hair, a dry humor, and slight awkwardness.

"What a unique voice! A very distinct tone you have."

I had no idea what that meant as I stood behind the microphone in the cold room behind the glass separating me from the warm control room, but I assumed it must be good.

Two days later, we had three songs that had been written and recorded. My demo was complete! We were feeling quite good about ourselves. Mission accomplished.

As we checked out of the hotel, my father came up with an idea: "I think we should get a video of you singing and playing the piano that we can include with the demo, and I think I know just the spot."

It sounded like a great idea. Until we pulled up to a grand piano showroom and my dad declared, "We're here!"

"Are you kidding? You want me to sing and play while you shoot a video in there?"

My mother was holding the camcorder, but she was clearly on my side of this discussion.

"Where else are you going to get a beautiful grand piano and those kinds of acoustics? Just trust me on this one," my dad said with complete confidence.

Reluctantly, I got out of the car, my mother and I staying far behind my dad as we entered the room and began wandering around as he spoke with the owner.

"We're set! We can record all we want!" he exclaimed walking toward us. Knowing this video could possibly help further my career, I put aside my embarrassment as I sat down at the nicest, black grand piano I could see. Ignoring the handful of people milling around the store, I began to sing.

School dance

Finally! I was allowed to go to my first school dance. I was still attending public school because there simply wasn't enough for my dad to do to keep me away.

As I entered the halls, I noticed the social committee putting up posters. It was a video dance and something immediately caught my eye—'N Sync. Who were these guys on the posters and why was it not the Backstreet Boys? I rushed up to see it closer and to find out who these imposters were, searching for any clues. I noticed a company name at the bottom of the poster—Trans Continental Records. I wrote it down and vowed to find out who they were.

After the dance had ended, all I could think about was this new group. With their promo tape in hand, I went home and headed straight to the computer.

Yes, I knew I had seen that name before, Trans Continental Records, the same company listed on the Backstreet Boys' CDs. That was who I needed to be searching for! With a few hours spent on the computer, I discovered the exciting fact. The company was based in Orlando, Florida. I had to go to Orlando!

The next day, I came racing down the stairs. Forget Sweden; this was huge, the biggest possible! "Mom, Dad, I found it! I found it! The record company that the Backstreet Boys and this new group 'N Sync are with. It's in Orlando!"

They knew where I was headed with this. Paper in hand, information written down, this was my golden ticket! "They have a number. You *have to* call them!"

My father took the paper, asked some questions, we discussed for a moment, and then he took the phone and said, "I guess it's worth a shot." He disappeared upstairs, phone in hand, and what seemed like the longest moments of my life slowly began to pass.

Finally reappearing, Dad reported, "They are interested in your demo and want us to send it to them!"

I couldn't believe it!

The invitation

We took photos against the white wall in our living room, wrote a biography, and sent the package. We thought to be safe we'd send copies to all of the major labels in Canada, as well as Trans Continental in Orlando. I had experienced small-scale Christian label interest a couple years earlier but had made the decision that pop music was where I could have the biggest influence.

Weeks passed and then it began to happen, letters in the mail from the major labels. "Thank you for your interest. At this time we are not looking for any artists in your genre and are going to pass." All the responses had come in; everyone had passed, except that we had not yet heard from Trans Continental.

"Dad, I think you should call them," I finally suggested.

"Well, it might be more of the same, but I guess it's worth a shot to see if they received your demo."

Again, he disappeared upstairs with the phone. I waited, tension filling in my stomach. This was my last chance—and honestly, the only one I really wanted. It was my dream company.

I could see the excitement in my dad's face as he bounded down the stairs. Something good had happened. My mother and I gathered round, urging him to tell us what had happened!

"They received the package! They like the package! They think you're great! And they've invited us to come to Orlando to meet with them and the company for a big benefit concert they are doing next weekend!"

Screams of joy! Jumping with excitement, hand in hand around the room! This was it!

And then my mom interjected some reality: "You can't go to Florida. We can't afford the trip."

And with that statement, the celebration came to a screeching halt. What did she mean, we can't afford it? This was my life's biggest dream! I was going to get to Florida one way or another.

Over the next few days, I worked on my dad. I knew he was on the fence; I could tell he really wanted to go. My mom was laying down the reality card pretty hard. The new house had cost a lot, and my career goals had already been distracting my dad's work and profits. We simply couldn't afford it. But when dreams and once-in-a-lifetime opportunities are involved, how can you not take the risk?

It was the night before the day we would have to leave. I had tried everything, and it didn't look as if we were going. I was distraught, unable to sleep. *How can life be this cruel?* I asked myself. The items I had planned to pack were in a pile ready to go. *Is there nothing else I can do?*

I had to pour out my heart and try one more time.

Dear Dad,

I realize that we don't have a lot of money right now, but there is never going to be a perfect time to do this. You don't get a lot of shots in life and I'm being offered one right now. It's a once-in-a-lifetime experience—and the only thing I want in the whole world. Please don't let money stand between me and my dreams. This could change everything. What are you going to do? Stay here and live on this farm forever, knowing that you never took the shot to give your daughter everything she ever wanted in life? Or take it and see what it does and how it changes our lives forever? I'm the last child in this family, and this is your last chance to do something great. Don't let it pass you by.

I've always thought of you as a man who was a visionary, someone who takes chances and dreams big. I'm waiting for you to take this one with me, or I'll lose all respect for who I thought you were and realize you're just like everyone else with no passion.

I'll be waiting, and packed, ready to go to Florida tomorrow.

I folded the letter and slipped it under my parents' bedroom door. I had done all that I could do. I said a prayer. I knew it was out of my hands now.

Chapter 4
Chasing the Dream

We rolled into the airport at 4:00 A.M. We'd been driving for two-and-a-half hours in the pitch black to make sure we would get on a stand-by flight from Winnipeg to Orlando, Florida. There was one flight leaving at 6:30 A.M., and we had to be the first two names on the list. My mother thought Dad and I were both crazy, but I couldn't hear her words through my excitement. It didn't matter to me if we didn't have enough money to pay for two standard tickets or a hotel when we got there—or even the airfare to get back. It just mattered that we got on that one flight today.

Once inside the airport, we rushed over to the ticket counter. We barely noticed that we were the only three people in the entire place besides the attendant. She told us that we had indeed made it as the first two names on the stand-by list but that she wouldn't be able to give us any tickets or seats until everyone else had checked in. The hours passed with agonizing slowness; other stand-by hopefuls sat down beside us and we waited.

"Would Mr. Glen Striemer and Naomi Striemer come to the ticket counter please?" The words we had been waiting for sounded loud and clear over the speakers. *We were to be on the flight! This was it! Orlando bound.* My mother, still shaking her head, told us we were crazy one more time and asked the question with no answer. "When are you coming back?"

"We're going to try for Monday," my dad replied. It was currently Friday morning.

Arriving in Orlando

As we stepped off the plane onto the walkway, we were greeted by a gust of warm, humid Florida air; it was a bit like a smothering bear hug.

We walked through the most beautiful airport I had ever seen. Everyone looked so happy and tanned. And then I saw it—beyond the tinted automatic doors that separated the baggage claim and the parking lot outside—a palm tree! My heart seemed to skip a beat as I walked up to the doors in awe. *A real palm tree,* I thought. *I'm looking at a real palm tree.*

The plan had worked, we had made it! Luggage in hand, warm air surrounding us—but now what? My dad told me to grab my suitcase, he grabbed his, and we started heading toward the transit city bus. Before I knew it, we were on board; this was my first bus ride. With the air conditioning blowing in our faces and my dad asking the driver what seemed like a hundred questions including, "Where can we get a great price on a hotel that is in a safe area?"

"I'm going to drive you to a street called International Drive. It's nothing but hotels for the tourists. If you can't find it there, you won't find it anywhere," the bus driver said.

Thirty minutes later, we were dropped off in tourist heaven. Palm trees galore, hotels lining the streets on each side, souvenir shops, mini golf courses, tropical flowers.

"Wait here with the suitcases," my dad said. "I'm going to see what the rates are in a few of these hotels."

It seemed like I was sitting there forever before he reappeared and said we'd have to keep looking farther down the street; these hotels were all too expensive. Hotel after hotel, block after block, it was the same story.

Finally, when we had reached what seemed like the end of the street, there was one last hotel on the other side. After walking so many blocks, I had little hope it would be the one, so I said I would wait there while my dad checked it out.

I could tell by the smile on his face as he emerged from the double doors that we'd found the place. The cost was only forty-five dollars a night because of the remodeling that was underway. What a blessing we had found.

I was surprised by the nice, clean room but even more surprised by the junglelike atmosphere in the center of the hotel where the pool was! We had really lucked out! Tropical trees and birds were everywhere.

"You should call Pierre, Dad, and find out the details for the concert tomorrow."

My dad thought it was a good idea and took his number to the pay phone in the lobby. While I sat waiting, thoughts raced through my head: *What should I wear? Who will I meet? What will I say?* I could hardly believe it was all happening.

Dad opened the door. "What did he say? What are the details?" I quickly asked.

But the look on Dad's face did not reveal a happy message. He was silent. "Something's wrong. What did he say, Dad? The concert was canceled, wasn't it?"

Finally Dad responded. "Bingo.

"The concert was postponed till next weekend. He said he'd forgotten that he had invited us and apologized that we'd come all this way. He suggested we enjoy the weather and a nice mini vacation."

"What! How could the concert be canceled? How could they do this? What are we going to do?"

My mother's words were starting to ring in our ears. How could we call Mom and tell her what had happened?

"I guess we'll have to sit out at the pool like the rest of the losers and try to get a tan," was my dad's response. In 55°F to 60°F weather. Baffled, we sat in silence. Then the phone rang. It was Pierre.

After speaking for a few minutes and jotting down notes, my dad hung up the phone, joy beaming from his face. "Pierre felt so bad that he's coming to pick us up to take us to the studio to meet Lou Pearlman and the team in forty minutes!"

This was even better than a concert! I was going to meet the owner of the record company!

Our trip to TransCon

A black van with the words "Trans Continental Records" painted on the side rolled into the parking lot waiting area. Our transportation

had arrived! *Let the dreams begin,* I thought, because I was now officially entering into so many of them I'd had. It was surreal to be sitting
in a vehicle I knew had picked up the Backstreet Boys from the airport
and driven them to the studio and was now driving me to what seemed
like my destiny.

After riding for fifteen minutes, we turned into an industrial section
of town with box buildings everywhere. The driver turned from street
to street until we parked outside of a plain long beige building. Just as
we opened the doors to get out, a light-blue Rolls-Royce pulled up to
park beside us.

"Let me introduce you to Lou," Pierre said as he stepped out of the
driver's seat. "Here he is now."

I had never seen a Rolls-Royce before; I didn't know if it was new or
old—but I knew it had to be worth a lot of money, more than a quarter million dollars to be exact. The name I recognized from reading it
so many times on the back of the Backstreet Boys and 'N Sync album
covers; I knew this was the man in charge.

He was a heavy man, not very tall, with pale-colored hair, glasses,
and pasty skin. He greeted us and led us inside the back door, where a
guard kept track of every person who came in and out. It was nothing
more than a hallway, but it had records covering the walls, platinum
and gold, with framed posters everywhere. We rounded the corner,
and I saw "Studio A" on a door. There Lou casually turned back to say,
"This is where we record a lot of our records."

I could hear music pumping through the walls. We were getting
closer to people too; I could hear voices talking. We turned into another hallway just as a blond, curly haired teenage boy came running
around the corner, with a teenybopper magazine in hand, yelling,
"Does anyone know how to read German?"

He stopped to give Lou a hug; they exchanged a few words about a
tour it appeared he had just come home from. I gathered, from their conversation, the tour had gone well and had taken place in Germany. It was
then that I was starting to figure it out; his face looked familiar, but why?

"I'm sorry for being rude. My name is Justin." His hand reached out
to shake mine.

"Hi, I'm Naomi."

And then it clicked, this was Justin Timberlake, the blond guy from 'N Sync. I was meeting a member of 'N Sync! In that moment I thought, *I can never leave this place, this is where I'm meant to be, it's a dream. How can a place be so wonderful and really exist?*

Justin continued down the hall, calling out, "Can anyone help me read this German interview we did?" As we walked in the opposite direction, more guys and gals were passing us in the hallway saying Hello—more members of 'N Sync and what must have been other boy and girl bands.

We ended up in what seemed like the entrance to the building—a lobby, a few couches, and a door leading into Lou Pearlman's office. We sat down on the black leather couch against the wall; the bustling excitement continuing outside the door, so Lou asked Pierre if he would shut it. I didn't want the door closed; I wanted to be a part of what was going on with all of the young people. It seemed so perfect.

Lou began asking questions: where was I from, what was my history of singing, is this what I wanted to do with my life? And finally, how did I get here?

Pierre interjected: "I spoke with her father, Glen, who had sent me a videotape of her singing and accompanying herself on the piano. I thought it was great, so I invited both of them to come down."

"Do you have this video?" Lou asked.

"Yes," my dad chimed in. "We brought a copy."

Lou asked Pierre to open the office door and invite everyone in the lobby, the hallway, and the dining area to come in to his office to watch this video. He wanted to get everyone's opinions. My palms began to sweat; I couldn't believe what was happening. Just yesterday I had been in minus 30°C, on a farm just dreaming of one day meeting these people and being able to sing for them, and here I was, twenty-four hours later, and it was about to happen.

As the video came on, something inside of me wanted to hide in fear that it wouldn't be well received or that one of the guys or gals would start talking or walk out. Instead, silence fell over the room. You could hear a pin drop as I began to sing "Foolish Games" on the video.

One of the guys from a band called C-Note pointed at me and asked, "Is this you singing?"

I quietly answered, "Yeah."

As the video played through to the end, the room had become so full that the door was packed with people leaning their heads in over the shoulders of other people. Knots had filled my stomach. *What will they think? What will they say?*

Applause filled the air, Lou asking the question above the noise, "What did you think?"

People were saying things like, "Wow, you're amazing!" and "That was so good." I was thrilled.

Lou ushered everyone back out of the room. It was time to talk business. "Can you see yourself living in Orlando, Florida?"

"Yes, of course," I answered without thinking it through

"I think we should sign her to Johnny [Wright]. I think she'd be perfect for him," Lou said to Pierre, who was already making the phone call. Just like Lou's name, I knew who Johnny was; he managed both Backstreet Boys and 'N Sync.

"Johnny is out of town until Monday." But we would be gone on Monday.

"Can you stay until Monday?" Lou asked.

"Well, we'll have to see what her mother says; we really can't stay long," my dad answered.

"Take her around the place; show her what we've got here," Lou instructed Pierre. We left his office.

The next hour was filled with stepping into the studios, saying Hello to the producers, and watching the artists recording. Then we crossed the parking lot to another building, where rehearsal space had been created in a warehouse. A band called Take 5 was rehearsing while a girl band called Innosense watched. The choreographer lead them through step after step, a few musicians were there, and a vocal coach. One boy kept trying over and over to hit one particular note. I couldn't understand why he couldn't realize he was under the note, he was flat. I leaned over to my dad to say just that.

We spent the next two days out by the pool and discovering Orlando through the one street our hotel was on. It had warmed up so the palm trees and the exotic birds fit into the scenery perfectly.

Monday rolled around; we couldn't stay another day. Dad learned that a check he was supposed to receive hadn't arrived, and that was part of the money he had planned to use to pay for our stand-by flight home. He couldn't pay for our flights plus bills that were due, or another night in the hotel if we couldn't find stand-by flights. We said a prayer that our trip home would all work out. Miraculously it did.

Leaving Manitoba

It didn't take long until the wheels were in motion. My mom was baffled at what was taking place: we had just moved into the newly renovated home, several projects still needed to be done to finish it—and here we were preparing to leave. My father had called his company's Orlando branch, where they had offered him a job on the spot with promises of perks and a better life. It seemed that all signs were pointing to this one direction—all signs but my mom's heart. She couldn't believe we would be saying Goodbye to a home she had envisioned growing old in.

We still discuss in great depth how this move came to be and how it actually ended up happening. Was it a fifteen-year-old moving her family to another country to pursue a dream, or was there Someone greater in control? Sometimes in life there are no answers, just doors that open and doors that close. But it seemed as if God had opened this door wide and was closing the other door behind us.

My father's company offered us a seven-day trip to visit Orlando; this time all three of us were going, expenses paid. We visited the office and the church, had dinner with the men my dad would work with, and looked for homes that we could move into.

A month later, a moving truck pulled into the yard. My mom's heart seemed broken; mine couldn't contain its joy. At that age, I wasn't able to understand her hesitation as we began loading the truck. To me, we were heading to paradise, the land of milk and honey where opportunity abounded. All we were leaving behind was a plot of land, a house, and a few trees. It was a rainy, muddy spring day, and my mom mentioned a time or two that the sky had opened up to cry her tears.

Our life in Orlando

We moved into a bungalow in a suburban neighborhood. Its highlight was the pool; the downside was the mere twelve feet of lawn in our backyard. It certainly wasn't twenty-five acres. In the heat of the day, it would feel like the house was stuck on a cement slab that was frying it like an egg.

Trips to TransCon became a weekly occurrence. It seemed Johnny Wright was never in town and neither was Lou. The bands were continuing to become more and more popular, and the demand for new up-and-coming bands was becoming more frantic, so everyone was swamped or traveling.

We would pull into the parking lot in my mom's old '85 white-and-red Chevy Silverado pickup with rust on the frame. I was always mortified and would sometimes hide my head below the windshield so members of the bands wouldn't know that the vehicle belonged to my family. My mom always said it was the best pickup around, but her statement didn't make me feel any better about it.

After months of getting the runaround, we were notified that Johnny was finally in town. We arrived at the building, anxious to meet him. I waited in the lobby until I was finally approached by his right-hand man, Doug Brown. He took me into one of the empty rehearsal spaces, a room I'd never been in before, and began asking me questions.

"Have you ever thought about being in a girl group?"

"No," I said. "I want to be a solo artist."

"Well, you see, I'm putting together this three-person female group, and I've got two of the girls now, and I think you would make a great final addition," he said.

"Well, I'm here today to talk to Johnny about being a solo artist, so I'm going to pass on this."

Doug looked at my mother, who was standing beside me. She shrugged her shoulders as if to say, "I'm not telling her what to do." He pulled out a piece of paper, wrote down a name and a phone number, and said, "Here is the number of one of the girls. Go see her; she's expecting you now. If after visiting with her, you still decide you don't want to be in a girl group, you can come back and meet with Johnny."

I was upset that he was trying to block me from seeing Johnny, but I realized that I didn't have a choice. I didn't dare make a bad impression, or Johnny would never see me. I would go meet these girls and then come back and tell Doug I wasn't interested.

As we walked down the hall, we passed Johnny sitting in his office. Of course, I had no idea that it was the last time I would see him for several years. Then it would be backstage at a Backstreet Boys concert, after he had launched his brand-new solo female act, Britney Spears— and I would be a distant memory of someone he was supposed to have met.

After my meeting with the girls, I called Doug to say I was still not interested, and from that day on Johnny was never available. I felt betrayed and manipulated and was determined to pursue music whether they were going to help me or not.

I discovered there was another studio in town, and I made an appointment to go there. The owner, Dexter, took me under his wing, somewhat, and began working on songs for me. He said I had an "original tone" that was very distinct and very much my own. He would call me to come in the studio here and there to record something; but it seemed the songs would never get finished. I was frustrated.

On occasion I would be in Studio B, which was Dexter's hideout, working on a song while Britney Spears or the Backstreet Boys would be with their entourage recording in Studio A, usually either with the Swedish producers I had dreamed of working with or with Mutt Lange.

I was far too shy to ever approach anyone, so I would usually avoid running into anyone. My mom, however, one day made "studio friends" with Britney's assistant, Felicia (the woman who traveled everywhere with Britney), as they both sat on the couch in the lounge room. My only encounter with Britney herself happened when I went to the lounge to ask my mom a question as she sat with Felicia and Britney. We were introduced and shook hands and said Hello; she seemed shy and so was I.

When we would leave the studio, making our way through the

small crowds of fans who had found out their favorite stars were at the studio, I felt like somebody, until we would make our way to that old pickup truck and get in. Yes, it was ours.

Finding my way to the big stage

If there was anything in Orlando, it was singing groups, boy bands, girl bands, boy and girl bands. The city was inundated; it seemed people had come from far and wide to join the phenomenon. I had to prove I wasn't going to get lost in the crowd, so I begged my dad to take on an alias, call show venues, and try to get me booked!

I found some dancers and began working with them on the three songs I had finally finished after a year and a half at Parc Studios. Thomas Harold, a.k.a. Dad, was successful in getting me bookings at the two main venues where TransCon would have their artists perform, House of Blues at Disney and Hard Rock Live at Universal's City Walk (which easily held 1,100 people). I was the only non–Trans Continental Records act that had been invited to perform at some of these concerts. I felt like the black sheep, sneaking my way in to prove myself.

It was at one of these concerts at the soundcheck that I ran into Doug Brown again. He was primping one of his boy-girl groups. The only words exchanged were brief. He asked how I was doing, and I said "Fine."

My entourage would consist of my parents and the dancers I'd found. In contrast, each TransCon act would come with so many people, it was hard to keep track: assistants, managers, and publicists all to tell the guys and girls how amazing they were and what big stars they were going to become. I found it all sickening at this point, although I was simultaneously a bit jealous that I wasn't on the inside of that circle.

I attended the after parties and hung out with everyone, but I never felt included. The parties were lavish, with no expenses spared to provide endless mountains of food and fountains of drinks. In contrast, I tried to present an act that was wholesome and felt the need to depend on God for money every day for a family who still didn't know where next month's rent would come from.

One of my best friends during this time was the daughter of Lou Pearlman's top business partner. We would have sleepovers and hang-outs, even going so far as having an overnight stay at Lou's mansion while both he and my parents were out of town. The members of LFO (Lyte Funky Ones) were there and a few of their friends. We wandered around the huge house, going from room to room. I felt like cameras were on us the whole time and kept one eye open the entire night as I slept in what I was told was JC Chasez's (from 'N Sync) room.

It seemed the kids were taught to act much older than they really were, alcohol flowed steadily, and drugs were rumored to be circulating. I continued to avoid all of it, as I never had an interest to become wasted. There was nothing in life that I was trying to escape from, and I didn't like the idea of not being in control. I watched and learned the behaviors of others. My focus wouldn't allow me to wander off track with such foolishness. Boys could wait as well.

A fan base had begun to build from the shows I was doing, and it wasn't long before a few of these fans had built fan sites for me on the Web. It was my music on one of these fan sites that led a London-based producer to contact me through e-mail, requesting that I listen to his music for consideration.

I was surprised and thought his music was quite good, but how would I get to London, England? I knew I needed someone who was serious about my career and not using me or the songs on my demo recordings to be sold to other artists. As the question hung in the air, I leapt at the opportunity to go to Atlanta with one of my new friends, who also happened to be AJ McLean's (Backstreet Boys member) best friend. I had spent time hanging out with AJ at his home with Mike on a few occasions, and Mike was driving to Atlanta, Georgia, to see them in concert. We would have full access, and I could possibly meet Nick Carter, the one member of Backstreet Boys whom I still had not met! I was seventeen years old now and surely old enough to decide whether to go on this road trip. Also, a songwriter named Andrew Fromm from New Jersey, with whom I had been communicating with over the phone, was going to be there!

The trip was long, the hotel room was nice with two double beds that I had made sure were requested. My friend Mike would sleep on his, and I would sleep in mine; there would be no crossing of those two islands that night.

The concert was a dream, walking backstage, seeing Johnny Wright, meeting Andrew Fromm, seeing AJ; but still no Nick Carter.

Heading to London

When I returned home, I found out that a London-based financial group wanting to launch a record label had contacted Dexter Redding, wanting him to fly to London, England, to discuss a partnership. I was the artist he was pitching to them to begin the process. And just like that, I had my ticket to London! All expenses paid for me and my mom for five days.

I quickly contacted the producer, and we began working on a song I could record while I was there. Back and forth the e-mails flew. I would send clips of songs I liked and why I liked them; he would send back clips of songs he was writing; I would say what I did and didn't like—and finally we had it! A beautiful piece of music that was lacking only the lyrics and melody, which we would finish when I got there.

We were greeted at the London airport by a bodyguard and chauffer. The limo was waiting outside to take us to our swanky downtown London hotel. Hours later, we were meeting with these businessmen. I never felt comfortable with them; they seemed shady to me. There was little talk of music, and it didn't seem like a legitimate music deal. I felt like a trophy. My mom and I were given the limo, the driver, and the bodyguard to sightsee around London. I believed it was so they could spy on us.

On day two, I made a meeting with Michael, the producer; he called his songwriter friend, Debbie, and we were set for 4:00 p.m. that afternoon to begin working on the song.

Even though it was only the second day in London, I was being pressured to make a decision about signing with this company. The room must have been costing seven hundred pounds an evening. But I wasn't impressed. Finally, Dexter and his work companion, Wesley, barged into our hotel room asking, "Are you going to sign with these men?" Immediately, something inside of me said *No,* and then I stated out loud, "No." The men then turned to my mother, demanding she change my mind! She said what she had said in the past: "I don't control what Naomi does; I don't make decisions for her."

With that they left. Forty minutes later, we received a phone call saying my trip had been shortened, and I was no longer needed in London. I would be flying out at 9:00 A.M. the following morning.

Quickly I phoned Michael and told him that we needed to write and record this song that night. I arrived at 5:00 P.M. at Michael's London flat on Kings Road. His studio occupied the second floor, which was also the location of his living room. It was London shab if there ever was such a thing, yet warm and inviting at the same time. I knew this recording would go well.

We worked through the night, recording the vocals between 2:00 and 4:00 A.M. He did a mixdown, and finally at 5:00 A.M., I had a CD of this song in my hand. It was the only song I'd recorded up to that time that showed my vocal range. It reminded me of my favorite artists, Céline, Whitney, and Mariah. I was filled with such joy knowing this song would lead me to great things. I was convinced this was exactly what I had needed to reach my next goal.

The limo picked us up, we grabbed our luggage at the hotel, and headed straight to the airport, not seeing or speaking to anyone else. My mother and I both knew something very special had just happened, and we couldn't wait to tell my dad.

Chapter 5
Entertaining the World

I spent the summer convincing my dad that all I needed in the whole world was to go back to London to continue writing songs with Michael. Our family may not have been financially stable, but I truly believed my dad could make anything happen, including this.

I began collecting pieces of music to e-mail Michael, so that we could begin writing that summer. It was part of my process; I would describe what type of songs I wanted and would include samples of drums, orchestration, or piano that illustrated the sound I was looking for. I had no doubts in my mind that I would be going back to London and that these musical creations would be the foundation of my future.

By the time my parents agreed to use their credit card to send my mom and me back to London on a seven-day trip in late September, Michael and I had written seven musical pieces that were waiting to be completed with lyrics and melody, and eventually recorded.

We touched down at Heathrow Airport, this time with no bodyguard or chauffeur to drive us around. I preferred the freedom of knowing this trip was under my control, and no one would be watching my every move. Excitement filled my heart as we entered the city in a cab, arriving at our bed and breakfast near Kings Road and stepping into the crisp fall air.

The writing began immediately; there was absolutely no time to waste. Michael had pulled together a team of talented songwriters and close friends and arranged a schedule of who would be at his home studio on what days to participate.

I'd never written songs in professional writing sessions like this before; I'd only witnessed songs being written at Parc Studios and had dabbled with a few things on my own. I watched carefully now, picking up techniques and tricks of the trade as we went along hour by hour and day by day. I had arrived with concepts and storylines of what each song had inspired within me, and it didn't take long before I was participating with the ever-evolving stories, the weaving of hooks, verses, pre-choruses, bridges, and intricate background vocal parts.

I quickly discovered that writing a song is like painting a picture; a magical formula needs to be brought together. The lyrics have to capture your heart and relate to the listener, not just you the writer, while at the same time appealing to the listener on a melodic level as well. The melody must convey what the words say and build and drop with the intention of what is being conveyed lyrically. There must be excitement, intensity, and vulnerability; but most important, there must be something that will stand out in the listener's mind and become embedded in their psyche to want to hear it again—and it all must be done in approximately three minutes and thirty seconds.

My mom and I would walk to the studio each morning around 10:00 A.M. on the busy Kings Road, passing all of the clothing shops, sometimes seeing the occasional British celebrity, and occasionally popping inside to look, but only if we had time. We would grab lunch in the tiny sandwich-to-go shops and quickly developed favorites. Roasted vegetable or basil, pine nut, avocado wrap was one, but none compared to what became our special-treat restaurant. My Old Dutch specialized in crepes of every kind imaginable, both sweet and savory and served on oversized round plates.

Once we arrived at the studio, it was time to work, and I would be stationed in that living-room studio with the tattered old couch, retired fireplace, and the two tall windows that looked down at the street below. Around 5:00 P.M., the patrons would begin gathering at the local pub, which happened to be one building over, but almost directly below us. For little breaks we would open the windows and look out, observing the crowds. By 2:00 A.M., it was always a bit rowdy outside, and we would struggle with the noise, trying all kinds of clever tricks to not get any of it in the recordings. During these days if I needed anything, Mom would run out to get it; often times she'd go and come back with treats for everyone without anyone asking for a thing. She was always thoughtful and refreshed the people in the room with her surprises.

When we had passed the halfway mark of our trip, the team knew we'd never get all of the songs written and recorded within our time frame; the trip simply had to be extended for a few more days. The call was made to Dad, and he miraculously agreed to allow the extra charges for us to extend our trip to a total of ten days once he heard the incredible progress we were making and how happy we were.

Our bed and breakfast was wonderful. They, too, had no problem extending our stay. The owners were friendly and every morning would offer us a big breakfast of muesli, oatmeal, toast, beans, eggs, and tomatoes—a classic London breakfast. Our room looked royal, with high canopy beds, antique furniture, fifteen-foot ceilings, and beautiful curtains. It couldn't have been more perfect.

As the days rolled on and the songs continued to take shape, an obvious excitement began to build within the team; we realized that we were creating something special and unique. Michael began to make a few phone calls, and one day a frail but bubbly guest appeared at our daily session. Her name was Michelle de Vries, and she was a music publisher. Anxious to play her what we had been working on, we stopped everything we were doing and pulled up the finished tracks on the computer. I wasn't entirely sure who she was or what she did or how she could help me, but I was glad to meet somebody else in the business and came to conclude she had to be somebody important. My hunch was validated when, after she listened through the material, she said, "If these songs turn out the way I think they're going to turn out, I'm going to be very pleased! Make sure you send them to me as soon as you're finished."

Once she had left, Michael told me she was a prominent person in the London music scene and had contacts everywhere, including the U.S. I bookmarked this in my mind and held tightly to the business card she had given me. I knew I must be in touch with her.

Back to the United States

When I stepped off the plane in Orlando, Florida, I had eight fully produced and fully finished songs in my hand. My entire future and career rested on these eight songs. A lot had been invested to produce them.

The songs divided into two categories: four songs that were truly original stylistically and had been carefully hand-crafted by Michael and myself, and four songs that were more typical of what was happening in music at that time.

I wasted no time in e-mailing Michelle DeVries to ask whether she had received the songs from Michael and what she thought of them. I also asked whether she could help me get a record deal. Her response would change my life forever.

Yes, she replied, she had received the songs. Yes, she thought they were incredible, amazing, original hits. And yes, she would introduce me to someone she thought could help me get a record deal. His name was Peter Lewit. He was an attorney at Davis Shapiro & Lewit, one of the most prominent entertainment law firms in New York City, and they just happened to be good friends.

After racing around our Florida bungalow with the news, I sat down with his e-mail address in hand. I had no time to waste. I had to contact this man immediately.

> Dear Mr. Lewit,
> My name is Naomi Striemer. I am a singer/songwriter. Michelle DeVries gave me your e-mail address. I would like to talk to you about my music career and getting a record deal. I have songs that I can send you.

A few days passed before I received his response.

> Naomi,
> Thank you for your e-mail. Would you be able to send me a demo of your music, a photo, and a biography? I will review it and get back to you.
> Sincerely,
> Peter

The package was carefully filled. One CD containing nine songs (eight new songs and one song from the first trip), one biography my dad and I carefully rewrote together, and three photos that had been taken in London.

A photographer friend, Richard Morava, famous for his pop star shots, had flown into London to document the last few days of the recording session. An impromptu photo shoot had been arranged, complete with a hairstylist and makeup artist. It had been my first official photo shoot, and I knew the photos would come in handy. The pictures had turned out great! And they graced the cover of my demo.

A few weeks went by; I heard nothing. Anxious to find out what Peter had thought, I gave him a phone call. Pacing the floor, I asked the receptionist if I could speak with Peter Lewit. I waited a few minutes, and then a friendly, positive-sounding voice, answered. I was relieved; he knew who I was! He said he had received the package and it was very nice. He thought the songs were great, the photos were great, and my story was unique. But . . . he'd really have to meet me in person before making a decision to represent me. He said he had been deceived by packages in the past. Was I coming to New York City anytime in the near future? he asked.

At the moment all I could think to say was, "Yes! Of course!" Somehow those words escaped my mouth, and I was making plans to meet with him at the law firm sometime at the end of February, which was only two months away.

The truth is I had been mentioning a trip to New York City to my dad because I had been given the contact information (by my friend from the Backstreet Boys concert, Andrew Fromm) for Céline Dion's vocal coach. It was a dream of mine to work with anyone who had worked with Céline Dion's voice. I just had to go do it! And now I had even more of a reason to really make the trip.

After much coaxing, pleading, plotting, and begging, my dad finally agreed. He would send my mom and me to New York City. But this was the last trip for my music that he could sponsor. The family simply couldn't continue spending so much on my career without solid, financially rewarding results.

I knew the pressure was on; I had hoped big before and had not received the totality of what I was trying to achieve. This time I knew it was going to be different though. I could just feel it. I knew Peter would work with me, and if he was as big and important as everyone said he was, he could get me my record deal!

I made plans to be in New York City for one week. I arranged to meet with Peter Lewit on Tuesday afternoon, the same day we arrived in the city.

When the big day arrived, Mom and I flew to New York, hired a cab, and headed for the office. Our suitcases were placed near the receptionist desk as we entered the make-it-or-break-it meeting. I was surprised to meet Peter. He was warm and friendly and clean-cut, but had rock star hair. His office was big and full of sunlight.

I sat down and began my pitch, which included every reason why he should represent me, why I was unique, and how I could fit into the marketplace. When I was finished, he looked at me and said, "I have never in my career heard an artist represent herself so well. You've sold me." When the hour-and-a-half-long meeting ended, I was told I would receive a phone call that evening from his assistant, and I would be given the names, numbers, and meeting times for the next week with the biggest record labels in New York City.

Over the next few days, my mother and I walked from one end of the city to the other. We saw fancy, grand, intimidating corporate offices while we visited RCA, Jive, J, Altantic, EMI, and Epic Records. We were invited to dinner with Peter and his beautiful attorney wife at a stylish vegetarian restaurant in the East Village. Peter reported that I had impressed many of the artist and repertoire people I had met. Now it was just a waiting game to see who would respond first.

On Friday afternoon when I got the call back from Jim Welch at Epic/Sony Records, I had a feeling this was it.

Nobody tells you how it is going to be. Partly because no one knows how it will be. Every story is unique, unfolding in just the way only that story can. My story was exceptionally rare. I wasn't aware of it at the time because I had such focus and determination; I thought I could believe anything into existence. I couldn't imagine anything standing in my way. The truth is, getting a record deal usually takes months with numerous meetings and showcases. I was one of the exceptions to this rule.

Making my first album

The phone calls and e-mails began several weeks before the ink was dry on the contract. There was so much excitement and buzz, we couldn't wait the full two months for the paperwork to be complete. I was asked to submit a dream list of songwriters and producers I would like to work with. I began by going through my favorite CD booklets and writing down each of the names of the people who had worked on my favorite songs. Once it was complete, I submitted it. In return, I received a list of songwriters and producers I should research that Jim, my artists and repertoire person, felt I would work well with.

On that list was a songwriter by the name of Peter Zizzo. He had written smash hits including "Only One Road" and "Misled," sung by Céline Dion. His was the name I responded to first. Could I really work with him? The answer was Yes, and not only Yes, but he lived in New York City, had already heard my music, and was interested in writing with me on my next trip to New York!

During April 2001, Mom and I were back on an airplane headed for New York City, but this time Dad was with us too. It was the trip to solidify everything we had worked so long and hard for. I was going to sign my first record deal, to become an official Sony recording artist.

We were picked up at LaGuardia Airport by a driver holding up a card with my name on it, taken to a black town car, and driven to a swanky hotel across the street from the World Trade Center. The room was a large business suite with two and a half rooms that looked at the Twin Towers. We were like three kids in a candy store. We didn't know what to do first!

The next morning we made our way to the law offices of Davis Shapiro & Lewit. It was time to sign the contract. The one that said I would have five hundred thousand dollars to spend on my first album, seven hundred fifty thousand dollars on my second, and one million dollars for my third. I would be given an upfront personal advance of fifty thousand dollars, and my faithful attorney, Peter Lewit, would be paid the same by Sony for securing the deal. I was happy with the paragraphs that stated I would have 50 percent creative control over the songs to appear on the album and the choosing of singles. It was an incredible contract. Peter had done well and given me a tremendous amount of clout as an eighteen-year-old stepping into her first deal.

From this meeting the three of us headed to more meetings, this time with three potential managers that Lewit had arranged. They all had very different styles, offices, and dispositions. The first was situated in a "hip" space, very trendy, and was currently working with several relatively unknown artists who were all unique. The second was in a high-rise. The office was cluttered, packed with what seemed like too much stuff. Paper was everywhere. There was no real style or "look." However, the man was nice, in his mid-thirties, and had just successfully launched Christina Aguilera into superstardom with her first album. He was currently going through legal proceedings with her as she had just fired him over imaging disagreements. The third meeting was in a clean, crisp, minimalist office. Through the window to the side of the man's desk was the Empire State Building lighting up the evening sky. He himself was clean-cut and in his early thirties. He was running the offices, which consisted of several managers as well as an Indie label, and he had no time for nonsense. He wanted to know if this could work between him and me. It wasn't ten minutes into our introductory conversation that my parents did what they do best, and began talking at the same time over me to explain a detail of my story. Once we had all finished the chatter, his response was, "Do you always do that?" This was the first meeting in which I felt the manager was not selling himself to me as the others had done. And I believed he should be; after all, I was the hot new artist in town.

The next day we continued our meetings, this time with business managers, the ones who handle an artist's money, I was told. They pay your bills; purchase your cars and homes; file your taxes—so you don't have to worry about it! They are put in place with the hopes of great returns and lots of money to handle, and ideally they will ensure you don't go broke in the process and can retire one day. We met with three business managers as well, and again, all very different in styles to choose from.

I was being given choices: the companies and individuals I would choose to mold my career according to what type of artist I was to become. At the time it didn't seem very life changing; but ultimately, every decision we make in life is major, whether we think so at the time or not.

I chose manager number two, with the messy and cluttered office who had proven success in launching a big-voiced female artist. And I went with the business manager who seemed warm and friendly, who had the most record plaques on the wall and trophies from his clients. It was showy and where I thought I belonged. Not in some office that seemed like a bank handling my money; ironic, I know.

Finally after all of the business had been completed and my dad had made friends with several of the cab drivers, it was time to begin the creative process. I was going to work with Peter Zizzo and write a song together!

My parents and I rode up the elevator together, walked to the studio door together, rang the intercom, came in, and sat down on the couch inside the lobby together. While we waited, I stared in awe at the Céline Dion records to commemorate and recognizing sales hanging on the wall, my eyes stopping at lyric sheets that had been framed with a message written on them. I got up for a closer look, and sure enough, it was "Only One Road" and Céline Dion's handwritten personal note to Peter, thanking him for writing such a beautiful song. I took the moment in. I was really here! I was really doing this!

Peter popped out of his studio door and invited us into his large studio with a grand piano sitting gracefully to one side of the room and a large picture window looking out at the city on the other. I was offered the office chair next to his and nearest the computer screens, and my parents sat at the back of the room. Then the chatter began! After fifteen minutes, Peter looked at my parents and said, "OK, we are officially about to begin, so I am going to ask you to leave." Everyone was shocked. We may have come in together, but we were certainly not staying together through this process. My mom had never left me in a writing session alone before, and my dad had never accompanied me during one. After the realization that Peter was not joking, my parents both exited the room saying they would be back in a few hours to check on me.

And so we began, immediately getting along and sharing story after story. Peter laughed in amazement of how organized I was for a teenage artist, having arrived with my lyric ideas inside a plastic folder. He said he had never seen anything like it. And after what seemed like an hour of doing nothing more than talking, the guitar came out and the melodies and ideas began to flow. We took the remainder of the week to write a song called "Spin." It would quickly become a label favorite. Peter and I discovered we worked well together, and my parents slowly accepted the fact that Peter had a way of working that he refused to compromise.

The New York City signing trip was complete. I had become a Sony artist; I had hired a manager and a business manager; I had written a potential hit song and received tens of thousands of dollars into my bank account. Life was good.

London: My second home

The e-mails between Jim and me continued with great gusto. We had whittled down a list of the top songwriters and potential producers we could think of. Music had been sent to each to review, and we waited to hear from each to book my flights and make my travel plans to meet them all respectively and, I hoped, begin working.

London was the destination of my first official writing trip. Six weeks was the length in time my mom and I would travel this time. My dad was excited but a bit apprehensive at being left alone, not being able to see my mom for such a lengthy time, while wishing he could be with us both. Even though I was eighteen, none of us could imagine my going without a full-time guardian.

My itinerary was sent to me a few days before our departure. I would be meeting with Marius de Vries, who was just coming off the set of the *Moulin Rouge* in Australia with Nicole Kidman, a project he had been working on for four years. I would meet with Matt Rowe, a producer famous for his work and songs sung by the Spice Girls, and Cameron McVey, the most obscure of the bunch but brilliantly talented in his own unique way.

London was beginning to feel like home as we entered the city for the third time. We had our familiar favorite spots, and we knew how to easily get around on the subway, known locally as the Tube. We were set!

The question I quickly learned I would be asked by every songwriter and producer was what vision I had as an artist. Who did I want to be, and what did I want to sound like? Everyone wanted artist references. For example, if this artist and that artist had a baby, it would sound like me! I then quickly learned that each of the writers and producers had already been given a certain amount of direction from Jim at the label, in case I was unable to express myself in the most accurate way. Perhaps my vision was a bit hazy. I knew what I wanted to become, but I thought it was clearly portrayed in the songs they had been presented with of my music.

Days of introductory meetings in all kinds of supercool and some-what secretive studios were flying by. Each time we walked up to a doorway that looked completely unassuming, as though it was nothing more than someone's flat, we would be buzzed in and realize it was a multimillion dollar recording facility where icons of famous artists had worked and recorded before.

Each person had his own style and his own space to inspire creativity that was very unique to them. My initial meeting with Marius de Vries took place in a studio that had a solarium as a meeting room, full of sunlight from every direction! We were scheduled back to his creative den that had temporarily been set up at a studio to do the actual writing together. It was much different from the first! It was down a dark cobblestone street; the entrance door was almost in an alleyway that reminded us of where we imagined Jack the Ripper had roamed decades before. The stairway led up four different flights of stairs in an old and very used studio with hallways and doors leading every which way, until finally we reached the very top floor—a literal den. The en-tire space was at Marius's disposal: it was a large room with a high, peak ceiling, with a small window at the very top, letting in very little natural light. The room was virtually empty except for the secondhand couch that sat against the far wall next to a door. That door led to a small, dark room filled with equipment from wall to wall. That was his creative space.

We worked there for the next week and half, bringing in various songwriters to accompany the sessions, working on new songs and ones he had already started before we had met, which he thought might suit me. It was a great learning experience, but we never had immediate energy connection such as I had with Michael and Peter in the past. The best way I could describe the relationship was "polite."

Matt Rowe had a comfy studio in a very "hip" area of London where many celebrities resided, such as Jude Law and Jimmy Page, whose home we passed by daily. My mom and I would walk the paved trail up a hill and over a grassy park into the little villagelike area to work with Matt. It was stunning to look over the vast city from the top of Primrose Hill.

A large comfy lounge area was strewn with couches; a TV and many other things to amuse oneself were available. Matt's room was on the second floor at the far end of the hall. On the way to the stairs, we would pass a very large recording room. I would look longingly into that room, wishing that I could one day do something of that magnitude, not yet realizing that a few months from this visit I would be, with a thirty-five-piece orchestra, recording songs for my record.

There were always fresh flowers and a plate of delightful fruit to greet us in Matt's room. I found out several days into our writing sessions that the fruit was intended for my mom and me to eat! I had assumed that the fruit was for him and the studio hands. Matt had many studio hands, engineers working their way up to get studio time in front of the computer. The producers called it "paying one's dues." Some would work for five years as errand boys and watching the studios at night before they'd ever get to press any buttons or actually use their engineering degrees. It was a rigorous program.

Finally, it was time to meet Cameron McVey. He, too, was nestled into the same area as Matt, only blocks away from each other, and good friends. His studio was unpredictable, occupied by an ever-changing flow of people. I never knew what to expect. I was introduced to his trusted engineer, Paul, who was also an amazing songwriter, and we began to work. Cameron would come up with some musical ideas with me and the engineer, we'd place them into the structure of a song, and then he would seat me in a private room, usually cluttered by books and equipment, and shut the door. I was to "find him" once I had completed what I thought should be the lyric to the song.

My second day into this process, which was very strange and somewhat cold, but exciting and adventurous all at the same time, I emerged from my seclusion only to find out I had missed some special visitors—Gwen Stefani and husband Gavin Rossdale! They were two people I absolutely admired. Why had no one come to get me? I learned they were good friends with Cameron and lived in the neighborhood; they frequently popped in to say Hello, although they didn't happen to return during my time in that studio.

On the last few days of my visit, I had asked if I could reunite with my original team, Michael and the gang down on Kings Road. The time was arranged and I was overjoyed to see those familiar faces once again after so much had happened! But this time there was an awkwardness; the energy had changed. We couldn't re-create what had happened during those magical first ten days together. It just seemed like a work session now.

We returned home to Orlando excited and exhausted. Dad had not fared well; he had developed lower back pain while we were away. It was good to be home, the family united once again.

We decided it was time to move out of our rented bungalow to a nicer, newer home, one that better reflected our newfound success. I phoned my business manager, who had allotted a certain amount of money I could spend on living each month (after we had taken care of the debt my career had cost up until this point). Together, my monthly allowance and my dad's income could provide a rather nice home.

We drove up to a two-story thirty-five-hundred-square-foot home on one acre of land tucked away behind some trees on Millionaire's Row. It was by no means the biggest house on the street or even close, but it was the most beautiful home we had ever lived in. I felt as if I had finally arrived.

Sweden-, Spain-, and Paris-bound

We stayed home for a month and a half before we flew out again on another six-week trip. This time we were headed to Sweden and Spain! I couldn't believe I would be stepping foot in Sweden. I had dreamt of working with the pop icons in Stockholm for a long time.

The airport was clean and crisp, with varnished wood finish on every wall. We stepped out into what we were told was some of the cleanest air on earth. Stockholm. It was beautiful and well kept, with almost entirely empty highways. We drove out into the country and to our hotel that looked like a government building surrounded by trees. Everything was so fresh. The people were so friendly. I was in love.

Our room overlooked the lake, a staging of seats, and a lawn in between. We soon came to learn those seats would fill up quickly in the evening for a summer series of plays put on by the community. We never did get to attend one of them. To reach the breakfast dining area, we walked down a marble hall on the main floor and then up some stairs to a rustically beautiful dining area. Multiple buffet tables were filled with a wide variety of foods. White finely pressed linens covered over every table. I would run to breakfast each morning to relive the experience.

On the first day, we were picked up by taxi and driven ten minutes down the road to the studio, which was housed in two adjoining houses that were quite grand looking. They both had been used to house wives of the king a few hundred years earlier. We were loaned bicycles and given a map that showed the route along the lake to get to and from the studio and our hotel. We never had to worry about how late the time was when we were leaving because it was summer! The sun never fully set! I knew immediately that Stockholm would be one of my favorite places on earth.

I will never forget roaming the streets of Stockholm with Mom on my day off, camera in hand, delighting at every turn, learning that the city was built on a series of islands connected by bridges. Nothing would top the evening when we went with the songwriters to a hilltop restaurant. We must have climbed a thousand stairs to reach it. The evening was late, but the sunset never faded; it shimmered over the old buildings as though we were part of a movie set or a painting.

Our weeks in Stockholm drew too quickly to an end, and we were off to Spain with a quick stop in London; passing through Valencia on our way to the tiny island of Ibiza, famous for its clubs. It was a stark contrast from where we had been. It was dry, and the grass brown. Rock walls covered the rolling hills that had been there for hundreds of years, and on tiny roads, even tinier cars traveled to and fro. We arrived at our hotel perched on the side of a hill, overlooking the water and city of white houses and buildings below. Our luggage had been lost! So the clothes we had lived in for what seemed like two days were the clothes we had to dine in. Jim had flown in from New York to meet us. He was excited to see me and hear how I was feeling. He had been listening to the songs as they had been written, and he was very pleased.

My mom's suitcase arrived two hours after we did, but mine did not. As we drove down to the city for dinner, I begged the cab driver to stop at a store so that I might buy a shirt to dine in and meet the next songwriter I would be working with. He did, and I emerged ten minutes later with a burgundy "I love Ibiza" T-shirt. It would have to do. At least it was clean!

We ate at the most beautiful restaurant, live music playing in the background and water lapping on the rocks while the sun slowly set. It was as truly beautiful as I had been told it would be.

On day two, our hotel was flooded by a huge rainstorm. It wasn't the only place that had flooded. The control room at the producer's villa had also leaked, and his equipment needed to dry out before we could begin to work. It meant Mom and I had a day off. But I was not thrilled with a day off. I wanted to work! When the sun broke through the clouds, we found a beach the locals had directed us to. It was the clear Mediterranean Sea, but I could hardly enjoy it. My mom said I was a workaholic and went in without me.

On day three, we were relocated to a private villa belonging to Mark Hill (Artful Dodger band). It would be more convenient to work with us nearby to make up for the lost time. It was the most beautiful Spanish home I had ever seen!

Pam Sheyne was flown in to join us. She had co-written Christina Aguilera's big hit "Genie in a Bottle," and she, too, stayed with us at the villa. It should have been an incredible experience, but I seemed to have a cloud looming over my head. I was beginning to put pressure on myself that I must deliver the hits for this record.

We left Spain and went back home for two months.

One final writing trip found us back in London to finish my writing sessions overseas. The songs were coming together, the album cuts were starting to be chosen, but we had to be sure we had enough to choose from. I went back to write some more with Matt Rowe and a few others, although schedules somehow had gotten crossed between Matt and Sony. He was taking a one-week holiday when we arrived. This meant Mom and I were in London with nothing to do for a week. We had already seen most of the sights, so we didn't know what we should do, until my trip planner at Sony suggested we hop over to Paris for the week. Why not? We had nothing to lose. She arranged the travel for us.

One week was simply not enough in Paris. We instantly fell in love! The Eiffel Tower, the famous cathedrals . . . the shopping! It was here that I purchased my first expensive dress! A Versace black-and-white cocktail dress I thought was just delightful. My mom was not entirely sold on the big purchase.

We returned to London, well rested and ready to work. Felix, one of our fun cowriters joined us for the session at Matt's studio. It was around noon on a Tuesday when we sat down to begin. Felix was walking around the hallway with his laptop in hand. He came in, sat on the couch beside me with a puzzled look on his face. "What's the matter? Is everything all right?" Matt asked. "Well, the strangest thing just happened. I'm checking the news and it appears a plane has flown into one of the Twin Towers in New York City."

Chapter 6
911

We sat glued to the television for what seemed like hours. After pondering the news headline for a few minutes, everyone in the room ran downstairs, gathering in the lounge to watch CNN. It wasn't long before all of the other sessions had cleared out of their rooms to join us. There was an eerie feeling that something was terribly wrong, even though the newscasters were trying to make sense of it while attempting not to alarm anyone or cause panic. We watched the second plane hit the second tower, stunned at what was unfolding before our eyes. It seemed as if the world collapsed along with the two iconic structures. No one could utter a word; shock and disbelief filled the room. What had just happened?

We stayed for a few more hours as if glued to our chairs, listening to experts piecing together how the towers had fallen, watching replay after replay, until finally we could not take anymore. It was time to gather our things and each head for home, and in our case, a hotel room, to attempt to reach our loved ones and business associates to learn of their safety.

The streets were empty; crowds had gathered at pubs to watch the television. No one could comprehend the events that had taken place, but each of us knew something had changed forever.

We made it back to our hotel room, got the calling card out, and began to dial numbers in an attempt to reach people. My dad was safe; we knew that. He had not left Florida, but hearing his voice was of great comfort. He had been most concerned of our whereabouts than anything else. My second call was to the Sony offices. Was everyone all right? I could not get through for hours; I received only busy signals. The phone lines were jammed. Finally, late in the evening, I tried the assistant's cell phone. Success! She was safe. She gave me a recap of who had been in the office, how it had unfolded, who was out of town, and what had transpired in the city. Suddenly, Chelsea blurted out, "I have been walking for hours, it is chaos. I am halfway across the bridge from Manhattan to Queens with thousands of other people. The roads are blocked. No one can get in or out. Everything has been shut down. I've been walking for such a long time. I don't know when I'll make it home." Now I could hear the exhaustion in her voice.

The next day Chelsea, the faithful assistant, gave us a call at the hotel. She had been trying from home to get us on the first flight out of England to the United States. She was having no success. All flights had been canceled coming into the United States. We would simply have to wait it out.

We called Matt Rowe and asked if he was going in to the studio that day; he said Yes because he didn't know what else to do. We reassembled the team to write the song we had planned to start that previous morning. The atmosphere was much different—no laughing or joking. We wrote what we were feeling—confused, upset, angry, and hurt. Within hours we had written an emotional song called "Don't Wanna Be Alone."

It took another day before Chelsea could book my mom and me on a flight leaving London's Heathrow Airport on Friday morning. What a sigh of relief we breathed. We would be going home! There is truly no greater feeling in a time of distress than to know you are going home to be reunited with your loved ones.

Friday morning finally arrived. Our cab driver was surprised we were headed to the airport, especially for a flight to the United States. Conspiracy theories proliferated, and it felt as though we would be flying into a war zone.

The tension while going through security was thick; people quietly prepared themselves to walk through the check points. Once we reached our gate, we noticed that everyone was scrutinizing the other passengers as potential terrorists. As we boarded the plane, we found our assigned seats on the exit row. That was OK. The man sitting next to us had facial features of someone from the Middle East. He had been the target of many concerned looks as we had boarded the plane, and now he was in the seat directly beside me. He seemed to have no luggage and no carry-on. He must have felt as stressed during that flight as the rest of the passengers.

During the five-and-a-half-hour flight, the passengers were silent, somber, and on edge; no one slept, no one laughed. Our plane was routed to fly directly over Manhattan. The pilot came over the loud speaker to announce that in a few minutes we would be able to see the smoke rising from where the Twin Towers had once stood. It was a burial ground, and we paid our respects.

Landing in Florida two hours later, we sighed with relief and comfort. We were home.

Continuing on

After a month of recovery, pieces of the plan were beginning to form once again. A trip had been scheduled for me to go to Miami to write with a hot up-and-comer, Chris Rodriguez a.k.a. C-Rod. It was an easy trip, and this time my dad could come with us! We all hopped in a rented vehicle and made the drive down to Miami.

None of us was expecting the resort welcome we received! A long lane lined with palm trees, a grand south Florida lobby covered in marble, Bentleys and Ferraris parked outside, and valet boys running to and fro. We had been booked at the Doral Country Club (where we learned golfer Tiger Woods had stayed only days before). It was one of the most prestigious golf course resorts in Florida and certainly a change from the historic European sites we had grown accustomed to.

I met Chris at his studio, a huge open industrial space with a grand piano at the back of the wide-open space. His recording room was tucked away behind a door near the bathroom. But we would write at the grand piano. That day I wanted to talk about the rich and the famous. Having seen so many wealthy people where we were staying, I couldn't help but think what their lives must be like behind closed doors. We wrote two songs that week—"Entertaining the World" and "Broken Pieces."

The traveling continued with my very first trip to London alone.

It was only weeks before Christmas; we had begun production on the new album, and my mom's passport was about to expire. Jim and I had made the final selection of the eleven or twelve songs that would appear on the album out of the thirty-three that had been written that summer. Marius de Vries had been chosen to produce the majority of the songs, his name being attached to production for Madonna and Björk and, of course, the very popular movie. His name on my album would give it a "cool" and modern endorsement.

I walked the city sidewalks, excited with my newfound freedom. I missed having my best friend and companion beside me, but the feeling of independence was exciting. I went to some of our favorite markets and shops to pick out Christmas gifts and little treats to take home. It wasn't until I began the recording process that I really wished I had someone with me. The work was much more focused and precise than the demo recordings had been.

The traveling continued into the next year. Peter Zizzo was scheduled to produce three of the four songs we had written together in New York City. I was making my way to his studio to hear a few new additions when I was joined by a shy young girl and her brother. She sat on the floor and crossed her legs. Peter introduced us, "Naomi meet Avril. Avril meet Naomi."

"I really like your songs. Peter played me some of your stuff when we were writing. It's cool," Avril said awkwardly.

Peter joined in, "Avril is making a record with BMG. I'll play you some of the stuff we've been working on."

We sat and listened to each other's songs again until her brother said they had to go. She waved goodbye and they left. The next time I would hear Avril Lavigne's music would be on the radio, at my hairdressers, four months later.

That same week another artist named Vanessa Carlton came into Peter's studio. It was her birthday and she was headed to a strip club. Peter and Vanessa were also making a record together. I was meeting all the girls who were intended to be my upcoming competition. Peter would share stories and tell me when each of their records was scheduled to be released and problems they had encountered along the way.

I felt pretty good. I had not encountered any problems with my album or record label.

Four of my original songs with Michael had been chosen for final production. I was recording vocals in New York to be sent to Marius in England. We were slowly nearing the finish line.

My next trip to New York was the big photo shoot for the album cover! I had spent many hours at the Sony offices discussing with my product manager, publicist, art director, and Jim what "look" we were going for and "who" I was going to be presented as. I naively thought that simply who I was, the real me, was adequate. But they were quite certain I needed to be defined. According to the team, I needed to be presented in a certain way—and I absolutely must have a "look." Countless e-mails about clothes had been sent. Special packages with makeup artists' and hairstylists' work sheets had been sent to me to narrow down exactly who would work on the photo shoot.

We had begun discussing first, second, and third singles, and the photos would have to reflect that as well. The communication speed had picked up a notch; I received a daily blizzard of e-mails and phone calls. One of my original songs titled "Radio On" had been sent out with its final production for radio testing and had ranked "Top 10 in Top 40" as a prediction of how it would do on the most popular mainstream charts. This was huge! We had almost a guaranteed smash hit. Somehow a second song had leaked online and had ended up number six on *Billboard*'s Top Downloaded Songs of the week before they removed it.

I arrived in New York with Mom and checked into the memorable Paramount Hotel. The photographer, makeup artist, hairstylist, fashion stylist, and location had all been scheduled. I was gleefully excited! Recording was wonderful and fun, but nothing would be as outstanding as a photo shoot! I had waited anxiously for months to see what I would be transformed into. I went first to a hair salon to get my hair colored; then on to the makeup artist located at the MAC cosmetic offices for a makeup test, and finally to the Sony offices to try on some test clothing for the committee.

Then the morning arrived! We headed down to the artsy end of

Manhattan, rode up an old elevator, and popped out into a large, well-lighted room with fifteen-foot ceilings and wood floors. So many people were already buzzing around, the backdrops and lighting had been set up, clothes were being steamed to remove wrinkles, and accessories of every kind were being laid out. Each specialist had a space claimed, and I was given an order in which to see each of them. Makeup was first, then hair, then styling. I loved every minute of it! As the morning wore on, it seemed more and more people from Sony were arriving. When they stood me behind the fan machine to begin the first test shots, I counted twenty Sony people in attendance.

Several outfits, makeup, and hair changes later, we were finished. The sun was setting on what had been a perfect day. And a good thing too—because it had cost twenty-two thousand dollars.

We stayed in New York to participate in the mixing and mastering of the album. All of my work in the studio was complete. I just needed to make sure the final sound was exactly what I had intended.

We went to the famous Hit Factory studios and were introduced to Tony Maserati. He was one of the top three audio engineers in the world. I was so honored he had accepted our request to mix my album. His studio was clean and impressive. Tony was a warm and stylish man who quickly became my friend.

Unlike most artists who come to the mixing session toward the last day, I went every day and sat there listening as he worked. In the process, I learned quite a bit about mixing and made a lifelong friend.

After twenty (it seemed) repetitions of listening to the same song, Tony turned to my mom and me and said, "I've been trying to figure this song out. It's not about a boy, is it?"

We both shook our heads, and I said, "No, it's about the battle between good and evil, about Jesus and the devil."

"I knew it!" he said, "I knew it was deeper and more complex than a boy-girl story."

From mixing we went on to mastering at Sterling Sound. Everything was top of the line. This was a hit record we were making!

At the end of that summer, seven hundred fifty thousand dollars had been spent on my album. We had gone over budget, but nobody seemed to notice or mind. The buzz had been building, and no one was concerned with the cost.

Music video

We began discussing the music video in the fall. There was tension beginning to build within our home. My dad wasn't sure he approved of the direction my team was heading with my first single release, with its title "Turning More Than My Radio On." He felt the song was suggestive and finally said he couldn't emotionally support me if that was my first single. His decision hit me like a wrecking ball. As I saw it, Dad was supposed to support me. I was his daughter, and we had traveled this long road together to get to this very point. How could he withdraw his approval from the direction my dreams were taking me?

He began to travel back and forth from Ontario to Florida for work. He had been telling us he felt he was being called back to Canada to work. I was dead set against going back. I absolutely would not go! And my mom was torn. She couldn't leave her barely twenty-year-old daughter alone in Florida at this pivotal point in her life and career.

My dad and I began speaking less and less frequently until our messages were strictly being conveyed through my mom. During this time, confusion had also begun to build within the label. They had switched the first single choice at the last minute before finalizing the music video. Now the more quirky dance single would introduce me, then the sure-thing pop single would follow to solidify my standing as an artist, followed by a ballad for the third single. They said the strategy was airtight. These changes in release strategy, along with the alienation from my dad, made me a bit uneasy.

Over Christmas the schedule was made for me to fly to Los Angeles in January to shoot my very first music video. It seemed as if we had spent months talking through ideas and concepts for the video. The plan was to shoot the video and finalize the album artwork. The wording for the booklet was already being written, and we would have plenty of time to finish before the first quarter release of my first single.

January rolled around, but not soon enough. I was anxious to get back to work. I sat in our large kitchen with my mom; Dad was in

Ontario again for a month or two. We were chitchatting as she put dishes away, discussing everything from life to the album to upcoming plans until she paused and asked, "If you had to choose between the second coming of Jesus and the release of your album, which would you choose to happen first?"

What? What kind of a question was that? "Why would you even ask such a thing?" I demanded.

"Well I'm just wondering where you're at," Mom responded.

I felt a bit insulted! Obviously, my answer was the Second Coming, but what a ridiculous question! Why would she feel the need to even ask me something like that? I explained that I was being a good steward with my time. We all had to do something here on earth, and we were supposed to do it to the best of our abilities—and that's what I was doing. I was following a worthwhile job until Jesus came again. I continued to explain that, of course, my album was my top priority, but I most certainly had my priorities straight with how I felt about God.

Frozen budgets

I received a phone call a few weeks later. I had been wondering why I hadn't received my travel itinerary for the Los Angeles trip. I had never been to Los Angeles before, and I couldn't wait to get on that plane! It wasn't like them to delay getting me somewhere to complete a task. It was Jim. He didn't sound like his energetic self. He said a bunch of crazy stuff was going on down at the label. People were freaking out; everyone was getting scared. It was all because the attack on the Twin Towers had frightened everyone.

The phone call left me confused. This was a billion-dollar company. Why were they freaking out? Hours later I received another phone call from my manager Steve. Things were worse than I had originally thought. "All the budgets have been frozen," he said. "Artists are getting kicked out of the studio, tours are being canceled, everything is on hold until they figure out what is going on—" I was in a state of shock. Surely this will blow over. It is clearly someone overreacting to something. He continued, "Including your music video. It's on hold. You're not going to Los Angeles right away. Just sit tight."

I received a call from my attorney later on that same week to say budgets had been frozen for the next two months. Nothing would be moving. This meant my first single release date was getting pushed back. Now I was becoming concerned because the advance money they had given me upon signing was running low. It was only supposed to tide me over until the release of the album—and now that was being pushed back! What was I supposed to do! I had only one month's worth of money left in my account. My attorney promised he would ask Sony for the second half of my advance because I had indeed delivered the record to them.

The end of a dream

It took two weeks before I heard from anyone again. Peter had secured me an additional sum of money to last me another two months. He told me to use it wisely because he doubted he could get another advance.

Another few weeks passed. I was contacting the offices, but no one was answering phone calls or e-mails. Steve had no information for me. I was sure it would eventually pass and things would get back to normal.

In March I received another phone call from Peter, my attorney. He said Polly Anthony, the president of Epic Records, had called him to apologize for the disruption this had caused. She said she wanted to send her regards to me and that she was "going to bat" for my album. I took this information to be good sign. Peter said she was going to meet soon with the presidents of Columbia/Sony and Sony itself to discuss how to proceed. She would have word in two weeks.

One day Peter called me saying he was in Orlando and asked if we could get together. I said, "Sure," excited to see a familiar face and to learn more of what was happening. He seemed to be the only one with information!

Hoping for good news, I anxiously entered the restaurant downtown to meet with Peter. We exchanged our courtesies and then came his message: "You should probably start considering who you want to take this album to."

"What do you mean?" I asked.

"Well, things aren't looking good," Peter explained. "You can't stay with Epic. It's a disaster over there. People are jumping ship. I spoke with Polly. She said if you walk, she will negotiate a good price for you to take your album."

I couldn't process what he was saying. "Leave Sony? I'm never leaving Sony. They are the only label I've ever wanted to be with. How can you say that? Everything is fine; it will go back to the way it was. We just have to wait longer."

He told me a second time, "You can't stay with Sony. You have to start making decisions. You can't waste time."

I left the meeting in a daze. I didn't want to hear what he said. I wanted to go back and erase everything. Why couldn't he fix it?

It took a few weeks before I called Peter to say, "Let's do it. Let's bring this album to a different label and release it. I don't want to wait any longer." And with that, my dream of producing an album with Sony vanished.

It was legally easy to leave the label thanks to a clause Peter had written into the contract. It stated that if my album were not released within six months of my delivering a finished product, I could walk away as a free agent. What we weren't expecting was for Polly to go back on her promise and ask for the entire seven hundred fifty thousand for another label to buy the album from Sony. No label was going to pay that amount of money for an album they had nothing to do with.

Rumors came through the grapevine before they were confirmed of who had quit, who was let go, and who was transferred. My entire team either was let go or quit. The glory days were over. Polly Anthony, the president, was let go two months after I walked away.

Instead of my album being released in May, I was hiding from friends for fear of being asked how it was going. I did not know how to respond. I had not yet fully processed the events that had just taken place. This was supposed to be the most joyous time of my life! But instead, it was quickly developing into one of the most painful.

With my last bit of money, I booked a trip to New York, telling

Peter I was ready to see labels. I asked Chelsea if I could stay with her in Queens. I didn't have a song to my name that Sony didn't own. They had taken everything. But I rationalized that I just needed to open more doors.

I began the meetings, and one after another the responses stated, "Well, you have no music. . . . We can't start with nothing! You have to have music. What would you like us to do?"

At end of the week, I met with Peter. I knew that I must fight in order to survive. I could not be kicked out of the game like this! As I walked out the door of Peter's office, I felt an urge to turn around. Without thinking, I said, "I'm going to get you an album, Peter. I'll have it to you by the end of this year. We can pitch it in the first quarter." I had no idea how I would achieve such a goal.

As I reached the busy street, I reached for my cell phone to call my dad. He had been in Ontario for two months. "Hello?" he said.

"Dad, how fast can you move us back to Canada?"

Chapter 7
Six Months of Mourning

It took two weeks for us to move out of Florida back to Canada. My dad found a home in the country that he said was pretty nice. The rent was affordable, and we heard it had a beautiful kitchen. The real bonus was that the owners didn't mind pets because I had accumulated quite a few along the way.

I didn't tell any friends we were leaving until the day the moving truck arrived. The truth is, I didn't want to speak to anyone. I was operating in a cloud where nothing seemed real. If I could have found a cave to hide in, I would have.

The haste of the move was for multiple reasons, one being that I didn't have enough money to pay for another month in the big white dream house or to pay my bills. For several months, Dad had been begging us to come back to Canada. He had begun to make a little life up there, so when the day came for the move, Dad felt joy while I felt anguish.

We drove in a caravan with a U-Haul moving truck and Mom's pickup, both towing our other vehicles. The entire way back I felt silent and numb. I was returning a failure, someone who had been defeated. I had left Canada five years earlier to make a name for myself, to prove I was going somewhere! After all, I had been voted "the most likely to become famous" at school. I had thought it was my destiny—so how could this failure have happened?

When we crossed the U.S.-Canadian border, we declared we were moving back. My parents gave up their green cards, and I gave up any hope of my dreams succeeding. I was penniless—with no career, no future, no record deal, and not a song to my name. My high school friends had gone to college to get degrees, but I had not. I was supposed to be jump-starting my career, bypassing the toil of being schooled for several years. I was supposed to be waving down below to all of them as I was flying high on the wings of success. But now I felt I was too old to start over, to try something new. I just simply wanted to die.

We drove the two hours into southern Ontario from the Niagara Falls border crossing. It was early summer and the fields were full of life. I, however, was not. Once the house was in view, Dad honked from the pickup truck behind us to indicate that we were home. As we pulled in, I managed to muster up just enough enthusiasm to say, "It's actually nice." I was surprised. In my mind we had been headed for a new home that would look exactly the way I was feeling—vacant.

We got out of the vehicles and walked inside. It was a beautiful home—very grand from the outside, sitting atop a little hill from the road, big old evergreen trees behind it, and fields on each side of the yard. The house was split into two parts; one half was the original brick farmhouse, and the other was the newer addition with blue siding. The entrance lead us through a living room with a fireplace, turning to the right and up two steps, we headed into the open kitchen with oak cabinets , and to the right of that, facing the yard, was a big solarium. It was perfect.

The first night in my new room, I stared at the ceiling wide awake. I was sure that everyone else was sleeping after a busy day of unpacking the truck. The silence allowed me to focus on the question, Why had this happened to me? I welcomed the night. It was the only time I allowed myself to reveal my suffering and despair. No one could hear my sobs, see my tears, or question my thoughts; I could display emotion while avoiding painful questions. My gut hurt in the morning from my sobbing, but with every brush of my hair I would remove the emotions from my face and head downstairs, trying to act as normally as possible. This became my nightly routine: embracing the moments of solitude while hiding behind a solemn, remote expression during the day.

I often watched the cars drive by and wondered what would happen if I walked out in front of them one day. I went from considering myself an important member of society to feeling rejected and unimportant. Often I felt that I had no purpose in the world, nothing I could do, and that I had lost the time to make something of myself. One day I sat in the Wal-Mart parking lot while my dad ran inside and my mom waited in the backseat. As I stared out the window, tears began streaming down my cheeks. I couldn't even feel the emotions that had caused them! Or identify why I was crying.

Over the course of the next few weeks, I turned from silence and self-pity to anger toward God. He was the One to blame; He had allowed this to happen to me; He could have stopped it if He had wanted—but He didn't! And I wanted to know why!

I felt brokenhearted and betrayed. I assumed that God had intentionally allowed this to happen to me, that He had deserted me. Wasn't I good enough? Didn't He love me? For weeks I continued to beg Him for answers.

My brother Nathan decided to come visit us for a few days at our new home in Ontario and booked a flight from Manitoba. I had seen him only once or twice in the previous five years because he had remained in Manitoba when we moved to Orlando. It took only a matter of days for him to sense something was off with me. It seemed that no one else had noticed—at least no one had said anything. Perhaps they were trying as hard as I was to ignore my disappointment and hope that, in time, I would recover on my own.

Nathan found me late one evening upstairs in the long room we had converted into a den and office, where both the keyboard and computer were situated. I was surprised to see him, assuming everyone had gone to bed. It was our first time alone since he'd arrived. Over the years, we had formed a close bond, an unspoken trust. It was a mutual understanding that he could share with me all of the troubles he was going through, and I would keep them to myself without judging him. Now it was my turn. I hadn't said a word about my emotional state—but I didn't have to. He knew. My first reaction was to deny it, but I realized that such a response would be pointless. So I told him the truth: my world had collapsed, and I didn't know what to do or how to handle it. Nathan asked whether Mom or Dad knew how hard I was struggling. I shrugged but admitted, "I don't think so."

"Well, you can't keep on pretending that nothing is wrong," he said. "Remember, you can always give me a call if you need to talk to someone.

You know I'm here for you. I'm your big brother. That's what big brothers do."

Just hearing those words of affirmation and concern helped me to believe there was a light at the end of the dark emotional tunnel.

Then one day I picked up a book my dad had given me a few years earlier. It was about the struggle between good and evil, God and the devil, Jesus and Lucifer. I felt compelled to begin reading it. Before I knew it, I was a quarter of the way through the book. It was serious but fascinating reading, and it diverted me from feeling sorry for myself.

Night after night I opened this book. I discovered that there was much more to life than me and my dreams; there was a constant battle raging behind the scenes! We were fighting a war most of us had never even become aware of. Whose side were we going to stand on? Who was winning the daily fight?

My conversations with God turned from questions of why I had been dealt such a terrible hand to how Jesus could endure this daily suffering, seeing what takes place every minute because of sin, yet still being willing to save us!

I felt passion and righteous indignation beginning to rise within me, and the only outlet I knew that could express these feelings was to write about it in song. Deep at night, after my family had retired to bed, I would go to the piano across the house and begin to interpret these emotions through those ivory keys. I would write the words that flowed so easily from my mind. Never had I been able to write independently before, with no individual aiding me. In the two years with Sony, I had never sat at the piano to compose a song.

In the nights that followed, I wrote "Stay With Me," a song that called through me as I sat on that piano bench looking out at the dark black night. "Lord, You cannot leave me," I prayed through the song. "You cannot leave me, please . . . I need You so desperately." I was clinging to Jesus like Jacob in the night.

Mending the broken pieces of my heart, I composed "Starting Gate," a song that would detail the flawed and tattered emotions I was feeling after soaring with the eagles and watching my counterparts take off into the sun to find success.

I wrote my conversations with God in "Live Through You" and expressed how the great controversy was continuing on in "End of Time."

But it wasn't until I received my first phone call from someone that I had previously worked with that I wrote what would become the most emotionally angst-ridden song of my life. I had sat in silence, not receiving so much as an e-mail from anyone for months! And then when it finally happened, it was to ask if my first single, "Turning More Than My Radio On"—the one that was going to guarantee my spot in music history—could be given to another blond, female pop singer on Sony, so she could release it as her first single.

My heart felt ripped out of my chest as I gathered myself just enough to utter the words, "No, I am not OK with that. I am sorry," before hanging up.

We were heading to town and as I got into the vehicle and the words were flying out of my mouth. "The audacity of those people to ask me such a thing! After ripping everything from me, they wanted to come back for more!"

At my dad's response, "Maybe you should give it to the girl; you might make some money from it," I burst into an emotional frenzy. Grabbing paper and pen, I continued to write until finally I put down the pen in exhaustion.

Later that evening, I took that notepad to the piano to see what that feeling would sound like, and my fingers began to compose a song called "Let Me Go." It wasn't hard finding the lyrics as they were strewn on page after page of that note pad. Finally, the release I so desperately needed came with that song.

My new album was complete.

Stepping ahead

I wondered who could produce this album with me. I hadn't been in contact with any of the people I had worked closely with in the previous two years. I had no money to travel to any of them either, and perhaps they would all be too busy working on signed artists. I needed a friend I could turn to, someone I trusted and worked well with; someone who would allow me to co-produce and share my thoughts on how it should sound.

Michael—Michael from London! That was it! We had experienced a few ups and downs, but I could trust Michael, and we worked well together.

I wrote an e-mail to him, explaining everything that had happened, where I was emotionally, and what I had in mind for our new project together. To my great joy, he responded! He had heard my story through the grapevine and was ready to work on this new project with me!

It felt a bit like old times again.

I began by recording versions of me singing the songs on the piano and sending them to him, followed by pieces of music I wanted the productions to sound like. I was more detailed than ever before; it had to be perfect. The drums had to imitate this or that song, the strings would need to add drama, excitement, and crescendos; every ounce of my pain, and the light that had shone through, would need to be expressed in every note.

Day in and day out we fired MP3s back and forth to each other. He would send me his interpretation of what I was describing, and I would send back a detailed e-mail discussing every note of every instrument and what was right and what was wrong and how it needed to be changed until finally, two months after my initial e-mail, we were finished with production on the songs.

I booked a six-hour block at a local studio in a nearby town, someone my dad had met through someone else. It was small, and had a very "home studio" feel to it, but the recording room was beautiful. Wood floors, clean lines, well lighted. It was good enough for me and just what I could afford. We had six hours to complete vocals on eleven songs. There would be three full takes of each song, with me singing from start to finish in performance mode. We would not be stopping to edit at any point, and once the lead vocals were complete, we would come back and do background vocals and extra parts. Once we had finished, the owner and engineer would burn them onto a disc for me and e-mail the files to Michael in London. That was the message I conveyed upon entering the studio. There would be no room for error. And there wasn't.

Somehow, by the end of that day, I had recorded my next album. It had taken one month of writing, two months of production, and six hours of vocals—costing me a total of $210.

Making a car payment

Somehow I had accomplished exactly what I had said I would a few months earlier, standing at the door of my attorney's office. How had it happened? By God pushing me every step of the way; it was truly a miracle album.

I put together artwork from what I had left from my Sony files. They weren't going to use any of it; I had been banned from releasing any of my Sony music, or even singing the songs for five years, the photos had probably been emptied out of someone's recycling bin by now. So I took what would have been my Epic album cover, that beautiful photo I loved that showed me looking into the distance with an empathetic look on my face, and made it my new album cover, which I titled *The Green Album*.

I had been cold calling people in radio (something I had never done before) and telling them my story and somehow got connected to a man who wanted to donate money to have three hundred copies of my album printed. It was an unexpected blessing out of nowhere.

While all of this was taking place, the reality of being broke was hitting hard. I didn't have enough money to buy a sandwich at a convenience store. What could I do? While I had been going through my great depression, I had toyed with the notion of giving up music all together and volunteering for an aid agency. I had even gone so far as to look up details on the volunteer program, but was quickly put off when it said that typically a five-year commitment was expected. And so here I was—needing to come up with ways I could earn money. What was I good at besides music?

I could be a vocal coach! I had learned from the best; I had all of my tapes from our previous sessions, and I could put an ad up in the local penny-saver paper.

As I wrote out the ad, humiliation filled my heart; I had to write intriguing copy to pique people's interest, but the biggest piece of recommendation I had also made me look like the biggest failure: "Former Sony Recording Artist Offers Vocal Lessons!" I couldn't afford to maintain my dignity. If I didn't make a car payment soon, I would lose my car, and then I literally would have lost everything that belonged to me.

I placed the ad and within a few weeks I had a handful of potential clients booking sessions with me. I was so nervous, being the introvert that I am. It would require me to be bold and outgoing, someone who could both critique and demand respect. It simply wasn't me. I was quiet, reserved, and polite; but somehow I would have to bring out another personality in order to make this work.

I saw a couple adults, who responded as if I were a child trying to bring knowledge to their learned years, and also a few children, who really didn't care to be there. It was awkward and frustrating, and I knew it was never going to work.

Back to the labels

It was time to contact Peter, my New York lawyer. It was late in the fall, and we could begin strategizing our approach for the first quarter of the new year to shop my *Green Album* to labels. My words played back in my mind—*"I'll get you a new album by the fall"*—and here I was, still shocked that I was doing just that.

I knew, without a doubt, that I had not made this record by my own strength and tenacity. It had been God, guiding and leading me through. I would still have been sobbing through the nights if the Lord had not picked me up and shoved the book that changed me into my hands, and then guided me to my piano to embark on a journey of creativity and honesty.

I discovered that God had used those darkest moments of my life to inspire me to push harder and reach further and build a strength that I did not know I was capable of. It was not because I knew it was taking place in those moments but because if I didn't move through it, I felt as though I might die, and the will to live and go on is strong in the human spirit. If I had not experienced the struggle, I would have never pushed myself to make that record of sheer raw emotion on my own, something I did not know I could do before it happened.

I found a deepening in my relationship with God. Now it was as if He were intimately connected to me in a way that no one could separate. He was my secret beloved strength, not just the God I prayed to about my struggles anymore; He was the God going through the struggle with me.

January arrived. This time instead of me flying to New York to visit with all of the labels in person, Peter decided to send the album to each of the artist and repertoire people to listen to and review. If they liked what they heard, they could fly me in for a meeting.

I was astonished by the response from my previous colleagues as they began listening to the new album. "I like this album better than the first one!" and, "Wow! I didn't know you were capable of singing like that!" "Where did this come from?" "It shows so much growth and development; you've really matured."

And finally I got the call I was anticipating with bated breath. Someone was interested in the album! He was an artist and repertoire at Jive Records who had wanted to sign me on my first go-around with the labels two and a half years earlier—before Sony had snatched me up. He had relocated to Universal Records since then, and he was the head of the Artist and Repertoire department. That meant he made the decisions; only the president could stop him from signing someone.

He thought the album had two or three hits on it, and he wanted me to come in to meet with him and the new president, L. A. Reid. His assistant called me to make travel arrangements. As I sat in the country, surrounded by agricultural fields, a moment of seeming redemption swept over me. The music world had not forgotten me! I wanted to cry with excitement over the thought of returning to my old life.

I was to expect a phone call two days later with a confirmed flight itinerary and the remainder of the details for the big meeting to solidify my new label home.

It was 10:20 A.M. when I received the call.

I was ready to take down all of the travel information, but instead heard devastating news. The assistant was talking nervously, almost in a whisper. "I am so sorry to be calling you like this. I don't know what to do. My boss, the head of A&R was just escorted out of the building with all of his personal belongings. He's been fired."

My heart sank. *It can't be true!* I thought. *This can't be happening to me again.*

But it was true, and it did happen. There would be no meeting, no new label, and no returning to my old life. After the initial disbelief wore off, I realized that if I had signed a deal with this man and he had been fired a few months later, I would have lost my entire new album to another label! Everything I had, once again, would have been gone.

I vowed to never let that situation happen to me again. I would build my name and make myself an entity the labels could not just toss around at will. I had to become an artist of value.

Chapter 8
Touring the Next Chapter

I began calling venues, bars, and clubs and quickly found out none of them were interested in booking me. I had no following of fans, which meant no "draw" to get people in so they could make money. I knew there had to be another way. As I sat to think about what else could be a possibility, it hit me. The bookstore! I loved bookstores and frequently visited them during my travels. Often I would see placards advertising an upcoming book reading with an author. That was it! If they accepted book authors to come in, read, and sell their books, why wouldn't they allow a singer to come in, play music, and sell CDs?

I called the biggest store in Toronto and asked who was in charge of booking authors and entertainers. The friendly voice on the other end said, "Oh, that would be Jeremy, our head of media relations. Let me get you his contact information." Without hesitation, I was on the phone with Jeremy, telling him my story. Within a few minutes, he said, "Let me e-mail you a few possible dates and a few names for more stores."

That was it! I was booked. It was a direct answer to prayer. I would be able to play at the Chapters/Indigo bookstores in Toronto in the hopes of selling CDs (to finally make my car payment) and gain an audience.

Behind the books

The first night was nerve-racking. Countless emotions ran through me as I unpacked the keyboard, nestled in between two aisles of books. My parents were arranging the CDs on the small table the store had provided for me. We had joked on the way there of "how the mighty have fallen" and if only "they could see me now." On the surface, they may have been jokes we could laugh about, but underneath, they were truths that we were trying to suppress.

This small opportunity was a double-sided coin. I was being given a golden opportunity to make something of myself as an artist and begin supporting myself financially from my art, while at the same time doing what I, as a singer, should have been doing all along, performing! Conversely, there was fear and wounded pride at the stark contrast I was facing that night as opposed to the debut I was scheduled to have almost a year earlier.

After everything was set up and ready to go, and my parents fully equipped with albums in hand to promote, it was time to begin singing for the customers roaming through the aisles, looking for that perfect book or simply killing some time. I closed my eyes and imagined I was in my room, alone, singing these songs.

The next time I opened my eyes, the several chairs the staff had set out nearby were now filled with people. My parents rushed up to me with handfuls of CDs to personalize and sign for people who had purchased them. I couldn't believe it! People liked my music, the music I had written! It was a feeling I had never experienced before.

I began to tell stories of my journey in between the songs and quickly learned this would draw even more people to gather around, many saying they thought it was simply music playing from the loud speakers, until they heard me talking! My parents would approach every person who came near to ask whether they liked the music and whether they would support me by purchasing an album. We went home that night with five hundred dollars in CD sales.

My spirit had been renewed; my heart had been refreshed. It was a little sign from God saying, Yes, you should be doing this. I knew I couldn't give up. I had never experienced being so close to my listeners before. I had always been on a stage with lights separating me from the audience. Now I had seen faces wet with tears as I sang my songs, and for the first time I felt a connection between the audience and me, the artist. It wasn't about jumping up on stage to look good and sound good; it was about uniting a soul and a spirit with lyrics and melody.

I did thirty-seven concerts in Chapters bookstores across southern

Ontario that summer in each of the major stores. We had grown accustomed to the routine that every weekend the three of us would pack into my vehicle and drive the average hour or two to get to the bookstores. We would always arrive unsure about how the evening would go, and every night we would leave beaming with joy. Regardless of whether it was a big night financially, there was always a special story we would share on the drive home. We were being blessed.

During the week I had picked up a summer job of high-bush blueberry picking. It was in an effort to save money to do a tour with my mom from one U.S. coast to the other. I had met a small-venue booking agent online who charged $250 to book a tour. He was lining up all of the venues and dates for me; I just had to show up to do them. I figured I would make enough from CD sales each night to cover the hotels and majority of the gas money. I had saved enough to get us started, with concerts in two cities on our way to New York City.

After two days of being on the road, weaving our way through the states to reach the Big Apple, we had only done two concerts, both at sports bars (which usually consisted of an audience of one or two each time). It was a clear decision my mom and I made. We decided it was a waste of time and money compared to what I could be doing back home with the Chapters shows. I had not sold one CD! I admitted that it seemed like we had fallen a few pegs walking into those empty, dark, depressing bars to play songs. The clientele was certainly a far cry from the upper-class, book-loving crowd we had grown accustomed to.

Our only lifesaver on the trip came at the last minute to open for Chris Issak, famous for his major hit "Wicked Game," in Cape Cod as a one time special event. They gave me a $750 guarantee for thirty minutes on stage and a chance to sell CDs. It was just what we needed as an extra boost for confidence and fuel.

We arrived to the unique circular indoor-outdoor venue under a permanent canvas that comfortably seated twenty-five hundred people. The stage was set at the bottom of the cascading seating plan with a rotating stage. My set went incredibly well and the audience had a huge reaction to my performance. Screams and applause sent a surge through me that this could be the beginning of something. Before my last song I invited the audience to join me at the merchandise booth for CDs before Chris took the stage, and they did, in throngs. My mom couldn't exchange the money for CDs fast enough for me to sign them. However we were drawing too much attention in the opinion of Mr. Isaak's manager who promptly shut us down fifteen mintes later in order for everyone to make their way back to their seats for Chris to take the stage. "You can come back and sell more after the concert," he told my mom. But that promise never came true. When we went back out to the "merch" table after the concert our items had been removed and replaced with only Chris, from one end to the other. With confusion my mom inquired only to be told "you had your time to sell." I vowed never to become a person like that, regardless of any level of success I might achieve.

We decided after the New York City gigs, which introduced us to a new side of the city we had not seen during our Sony travel days, that we would head home and resume what we had been doing, and then I would save up enough money for us to go to Los Angeles one day.

Chapter 9
Safe-House

Out of the clear blue, I decided to do an open-mic night in Toronto. We had spent the day doing this and that and had driven by a trendy music venue with a sign in the window advertising for that evening's event.

I waited my turn and finally hit the stage around 9:30 p.m. to do two songs on the keyboard. I had come to conclude that I was the only person performing who had ever been signed by a major label—or any label—but it really didn't matter. We were all just trying to make it now anyway. I left the stage to a great response. I quickly returned to sit with my parents, but within minutes I was being approached by a man who had been sitting with a group of people nearby. He gave me his business card and said he owned an Indie label in Toronto. His name was Anthony, and aside from owning an Indie label, he said he was in finance. He introduced himself to my parents, and we arranged a meeting at his office and home studio the following week.

I came prepared with a proposed budget in hand, two hundred thousand dollars, the amount I needed to release my album in Canada. I didn't want to be messing around with wannabes. We drove up to a massive, million-dollar house in a ritzy suburb of Toronto. A Ferrari sat out front to greet us. We parked and were welcomed at the door by Anthony.

After two hours of talking and getting a full tour of the house and studio, it was time to leave. I handed Anthony my proposal and he didn't flinch; instead, he quickly responded with, "Yeah, sure. Looks good." It was as though I was presenting him with a box of Girl Scout cookies. Little did I know that the next two months would be the most terrifying of my life.

After spending thousands of dollars on things that Anthony could control, such as re-recording his favorite songs from *The Green Album* in his studio with his producers, which made them sound terrible, I said it was my turn to dictate the spending. If we were making a new album, I would need a new album cover. So he flew me to New York City to do a photo shoot, which I made sure was productive by meeting a contact I had made. Douglas was a modeling rep, who signed me up with Elite Models Celebrity Division. Regardless of this, I felt as though the project was completely out of control, and it didn't feel as though it was moving in any particular direction.

Upon my return to Canada, it didn't take long for me to discover Anthony's business was not "finance" in the way most people define the term! I had somehow gotten myself mixed up with the Persian Mafia, and Anthony was the boss for Canada!

I didn't know what to do. I couldn't express that I knew, although it was seemingly being boldly brought to my attention. I had signed contracts with this man, and had spent his money, which I thought was part of a record budget for this new label he was launching! I couldn't just walk away.

One evening while at the studio after a group of people had just left, I was braggingly told that I had just met the son of the Chinese mob leader in Canada, who lived in Montreal and was Anthony's drug contact for import and export. I was asked if I wanted to tour the basement to see how they communicated their shipments to avoid being detected. I accepted out of fear of revealing that secretly I was panicking and questioning whether I should go to the police. I really didn't feel as though I had the option to say No. We went down the stairs into the basement, where and I immediately noticed several cages covered with black cloth.

"Pigeons!" Anthony laughed. "We use homing pigeons." He went on to explain the method of placing a tiny message in a pouch on the bird and then allowing it to fly back to its original departure point. "We have to keep them in the dark so that they don't create a new place of origin."

I should have run that evening and never returned, but I did not.

Perhaps it was fear of discovery that I knew something I shouldn't, and then being punished for it. Or perhaps a part of me clung to the hope that I was reading into things and somehow my album would miraculously be released and I could ignore everything.

A week later I entered the gates to the property, parked my car, and walked through the front door. The usual entourage was in the kitchen, which overlooked the backyard; they were lounging around, which was normal. I wondered if they ever did anything productive, and then I realized that I probably wouldn't want to know.

Anthony strolled in a few moments later with two women, one under each arm. He was a typical rich, danger-loving, thrill-seeking playboy in his mid-thirties with an overly confident attitude, one in which he was always right, and his word was never to be contradicted.

Anthony, with two of his men, had kidnapped his ex-girlfriend from her aunt's cottage (where I found out her family had tried to hide her) and had driven her all the way from Montreal to his house in Toronto, where she had been locked in one of the bedrooms. He held her there until she signed over some legal documents that Anthony had originally placed in her name for safe keeping (including that very house and his beloved Ferrari). They had dated for five years before breaking up earlier that summer.

I learned all this within forty-five minutes while hanging out in the kitchen, waiting for the producer to arrive. Anthony was not upset that I was being informed: he was proud and shared more of the details openly; for example, her parents had screamed for mercy as they had been tied to chairs in their home while Anthony asked where their daughter was hiding. With a smile and a laughing tone of voice, Anthony explained that such behavior was appropriate because he simply wanted the ex-girlfriend to cooperate and return what belonged to him. "What was so wrong with that?" he asked. She had been protecting the assets from the authorities only so that he could stay under the radar.

All I could think of in that moment was the contract we had signed and the money he had spent on my career. *How can I get out without this becoming my fate!* I took comfort in the fact that he did not know the location of my parents' home, although I admitted that it would not be difficult for him to find out.

I tried to recall everything that I had observed in his personality. There had to be something that he held respect for, something he looked upon as having greater authority and power than himself.

I went home terrified. Confiding in my parents, I admitted, "You have no idea what is going on at Anthony's house!" And as I began to tell them everything I had heard and seen, my parents became outraged! They demanded to know how I could have let this go on so long. Why hadn't I run at the first sign of trouble?

I waited for the phone call I knew I would receive from Anthony, the one asking why I had not been by the studio in nearly a week. And finally it came. I had come to conclude that the only area Anthony held any respect for was the authority of a parent. I was quite sure that this was my only way to make him stop pursuing me and enable me to walk away from any business ties with him. I calmly told him, over the phone, that my parents disapproved of my associating with him and his household. I was no longer allowed to step foot on his property.

Somehow a miracle happened because he replied, "I will honor this, because I know one day I will change their minds."

We all breathed a sigh of relief! The nightmare was over, and we could begin to wipe it from our memories. It was only a few months later that Anthony contacted me again. His house had been in the local news. A rival mob had invaded, and everyone in the house at that time had been tortured in an effort to find where the safe containing millions of dollars was hidden. Loss of life would have continued if a neighbor had not heard screaming and gun shots and called the police. As it turned out, Anthony was not in the house. He had been out on a date, arriving on the scene only after police cars and ambulances filled his front yard. He narrowly avoided jail because the police concluded it was an attempted robbery.

I wouldn't hear from Anthony for another two years, although I continued to look over my shoulder, unsure of whether I would run in to him. It remained one of my greatest fears until I received an e-mail from him, revealing that he had been convicted of his crimes and was serving time in prison. The e-mail seemed to be a confession of sorts.

He was aware that I was a Christian; perhaps it was his attempt at redemption.

Westward bound

That fall, once I was clear from Anthony, I had gone back to do one or two last concerts at Chapters before the season was finished. Little did I know one of those shows would open the door for me to move to Los Angeles.

A Canadian television producer walked through the double doors of Chapters that brisk Saturday night, and as he strolled through the rows of books, something caught his ear, and he moved toward it. He had heard me singing and had come over to purchase a CD. As my mom began to chat with him, he gave her a business card with the instructions that I needed to contact him.

We examined that card before leaving the parking lot that night. It revealed that he was a producer for a television series on CBC, the Canadian Broadcast Centre. This contact could be huge! And in only a matter of minutes, we all began to list dozens of possibilities that he might want me to contact him about. It could be anything!

My parents had experienced dozens of conversations with fascinating people during the Chapters tour—rocket scientists, lawyers, entrepreneurs—but none as exciting as this one.

I e-mailed the producer a few days later, so as to not seem anxious, and with his response he gave us his reason for contact. His TV show was looking for a new theme song, and he thought perhaps I could submit something for it.

He had his office send me a DVD with several episodes on it that I could watch and become familiar. The show was called *This Is Wonderland,* and they were looking for something fun, perhaps a touch ironic, but definitely positive. I knew I had *just* the song. I e-mailed him my choice, and I had a gut feeling it had to be the one.

A few weeks later, I received a phone call from the producer. The tone of his voice made me think it was positive. He began, "Out of seventy submissions, we narrowed it down to twenty-five . . . and yours made it through. Then we narrowed it down to the top ten, and yours made it through again!" He paused. I thought, *Oh no, I made the top ten, but they didn't pick mine.* A tinge of sadness went through my heart, until he continued, "After we narrowed it down to our top three songs, it was unanimous. We've chosen your song as the new theme for *This Is Wonderland.* Congratulations!"

I was blown away! Still clutching the phone while saying "Thank you," my parents and I danced and hugged around the room.

The song was being placed for thirty thousand dollars into the show! That meant that after the co-writer's cut and my lawyer's fees, I would be receiving fifteen thousand dollars for one moment of serendipity in a bookstore.

The world had opened up to me once again. My music had proven itself! I could make a living as a musician; this affirmation was what I needed to experience. My mom came to me one day soon after and said, "I think you should use this money to move to Los Angeles, where you can continue to pursue your dreams." I couldn't believe she was not only saying that, but that she was also giving me her blessing.

I had been yearning to make the move back to the United States in pursuit of my dreams. I knew I couldn't go back to New York City; every corner reminded me of heartbreak. So I had set my hopes on Los Angeles. It had more affordable housing, roads to drive on, and was warm year round! Most important, it could be a fresh start for me. The only difficult part would be leaving Mom and Dad. I was nearly twenty-two years old, but in every child's life there comes a time for leaving home—and this was my time.

What was scheduled to be my final Chapters concert was canceled due to weather conditions. A blizzard had hit, and there was no way anyone was getting near the store. I was saddened; it was supposed to be my very last show on this life-changing tour. I had looked forward sentimentally to this last concert. My whole self-confidence, income, and vision had been reborn in those stores. In addition to my nostalgia, a group of fans I had gained during these months had been waiting anxiously for this last concert. I absolutely had to make it up before leaving, so we scheduled it for the last Saturday night in December. Mom and I planned to begin the drive to Los Angeles in my car on January 15.

The show was like none I had ever done at Chapters before. It was at the largest store in downtown Toronto. They had set up a tiny stage for me on the second floor overlooking the streets below. It seemed as though hundreds of people had come and crowded round, and new ones were being added by the minute. I played for two hours without stopping and continued for another twenty minutes with encores. It was a total love-in we were experiencing. I thought perhaps we were going to run out of CDs to sell. Finally, I simply had to stop playing, if only for the sanity of the staff members, and I left the stage.

Family members were crowded around as I signed the final albums that had been purchased. Slowly people began to leave as we packed up. One man, I noticed, had been lingering for a while. He was watching us, but not approaching us. I thought it was quite strange. He was with a cute brunette girl who seemed to be his date; he had a small frame and an arched, pointed nose; he wore blue jeans and white running shoes. I couldn't figure out what he wanted. As we picked up our things to leave, he finally approached.

"Hello, my name is Steven Nowack. I work in finance and own an Indie label. What are you doing with the rest of your life?"

Chapter 10
Hollywood Walk of Fame

Little did I know that Nowack was a man of great conviction. It seemed that he could persuade anyone of anything, including the government, celebrities, diplomats and potentially me. Later I would be told a story of how Nowack became stuck in Switzerland. After losing his passport while there on business (and needing to fly home the next day for a meeting), his threats that he would sue and cause media havoc if he, as a Canadian citizen, couldn't get a passport replaced within twenty-fours, ended up producing a letter from the Canadian prime minister's office, a passport, and him on a plane the next day.

I agreed to give him nothing more than my e-mail address. I didn't recognize any of the names he mentioned in the music business, but I also didn't want to be rude. In my mind he was another elaborate dreamer, without a clue how the music business worked. My initial instinct should have been my guide, but instead my interest was piqued.

I received an e-mail two days later, requesting that we speak on the phone. He was very sincere that he was not joking when he said he was a hedge-fund owner and had wanted to start a record label. He'd been waiting only to find the right artist, and he was 100 percent convinced I was the artist he had been searching for.

Going with my gut, I declined twice. Why should I get involved with another wannabe trying to jump on board something he knew nothing about? I wasn't interested in redefining the wheel. I simply wanted to be an artist and work with people who had been in the business, legitimately, for several years—people who knew what they were doing. But at the same time, I couldn't let a possible once-in-a-lifetime opportunity pass me by. I agreed to a phone call that led to a few in-person meetings after he told me that he was in Phoenix, Arizona, where he had just enjoyed dinner with Stevie Nicks (Fleetwood Mac) and played her my music (after telling her everything he knew about me). The bait at the end of the fishing line was that he would tell me what she thought of me and my music only if I agreed to dinner to discuss a business partnership. Curiosity had the best of me. I agreed.

Three meetings later, I was sitting with Steven and my father at a diner in downtown Toronto at midnight, discussing how exactly this agreement would work. He had all of the finances in place—according to what he said—and I had the knowledge of how the music business worked and the talent. With his finances and my expertise, it should work splendidly. It just seemed too good to be true, and by now I was well aware of Nowack's persistence. I had turned down his deal offer once and received a barrage of nonstop phone calls for three hours until I finally agreed to speak with him. My mother was dead set against any kind of business arrangement with him; she thought he was a crazy person, straight from the get-go. But the truth is that half of the people in the music industry are crazy!

We agreed to give it a go, but only under my terms, and I would draw up a loose agreement the following week. Finally, at 2:00 A.M., as we walked out onto the street, my father, obviously with my mom's warning ringing in his ears, finally said, "How do we know that after we leave you tonight, a van isn't going to pull up with two men in white coats who are going to put you into a straitjacket and say, 'It was great that you had a lovely evening, Steven, but now it is time to go back to the hospital'?"

Steven laughingly said, "I guess you don't know!"

Westbound

My mom and I got into my car. It was January, freezing cold, and snow on the ground. The car was packed tightly from the floor to the ceiling. We were headed to Los Angeles, a three-day drive, to find me a new life, a new home, and a new beginning. My dad, standing in the yard, looked sad as we drove away. His last words, before our prayer for safety, were to ask if I really needed to go. I knew it was breaking his heart.

Nowack had been put on the backburner. With the money I had earned from the CBC placement of my song "Perfect (When I Grow Up)," I felt I could find an apartment in Los Angeles and begin forging ahead once again. In the worst case scenario, if nothing opened up right away, I could sing in bookstores again. Our not knowing Steven and how relentless he was made us think that we had seen the last of him. That illusion was short lived. A phone call as we were leaving the Grand Canyon tourist overlook notified us that he was already in Los Angeles, waiting to congratulate me on the deal upon our arrival!

We drove in to Los Angeles, both having contracted some sort of a flu virus, and went to our meeting with Steven at a beautiful, elite hotel, where many of the A-list celebrities stayed. Steven must have recognized our exhaustion because he immediately booked us a room for the night.

He had the contract in hand, two copies, one for me and one for him; no lawyers had been involved in putting it together. I had attempted to ask Peter Lewit to review it, but he had come back with a dreary, "I can't endorse this contract. I can't touch it. It's the equivalent to something scribbled on a napkin. There is nothing legal about it." He had continued, "If you sign this, you are either going to ruin your career, or be the most lucrative superstar who has ever lived. It's ridiculous."

I had added safety clauses within the contract, which consisted of the entire last page of the four-page agreement. Each stated a performance stipulation that Nowack would have to achieve in order for me to renew another year after the first. They included radio airplay—top 40 radio airplay in twenty-five of the largest markets in the U.S.; distribution—the album must be distributed by a major company or carried in-store by five top retail chains; media; and a few other things—like 25 percent of all net profits. That would be more than any artist, other than Madonna, had ever made. The most important immediate stipulation was the one that secured my financial situation for at least twelve months until renewal (at which point it would continue). After my last fall from an empire, where I was left penniless, due to a lump sum and nothing thereafter, I now stuck to my guns when it came to an advance. I said I would agree to work with Nowack only if he agreed to pay me three thousand dollars per month as an ongoing advance until the contract was terminated (up to five years later). All of this was in the contract he held in his hands.

Miserable with fever, I signed it, and my mother, also sick with fever, signed, as the witness. A piece of me believed that anyone who pursued something to this extent must have the tenacity to do something great with it. And if he could convince me, he could probably convince the entire world about my talent. And I was right—he certainly would try.

Over the course of the next three years, Nowack would visit hundreds of radio stations on my behalf and meet with some of the most powerful people in the music business, only to be told that in order to secure a top-10 single in top-40 radio, he would have to pay a hundred thousand dollars to a guy in a back alley who didn't give his name. This would prompt him to sneak passed the highest level of security to enter an elite music party (famous around the world and boasting a supersecret VIP guest list) in order to get face time with a revolutionary record CEO he admired, to ask for help and advice. Nowack truly had unyielding persistence and simply did not believe that any restrictions were attached to the word No.

He settled in Los Angeles for a few weeks to make some headway into our new venture. Within days my mom and I were meeting Nowack at a famous recording studio where oodles of Hollywood stories and stars had been created. We were there to meet American Idol's Randy Jackson, a resident of the studio. Yes, Nowack knew Jackson; they had done financial business together. It was the validation we needed, to finally meet someone Nowack had spoken about. Perhaps some of his stories (if not all)—such as touring on and off with Steven Tyler of Aerosmith—were true!

In search of a producer

Walking through the lobby of Le Parc Suite Hotel in West Hollywood, Nowack spotted someone who looked important and successful. Never one to waste an opportunity, he approached the man to ask what he did. Five minutes later, they were in Nowack's rental car (which doubled as his office) playing my *Green Album,* and I was receiving a phone call asking if I'd ever heard of Mario Winans.

"Of course. He had the most-played song on the radio in 2004, 'I Don't Wanna Know,' " I answered. "It sampled Enya's music and featured Sean 'Puff Daddy' Combs."

"That's right. Get ready, 'cause you're going to meet him in twenty minutes," Steven said.

Our impromptu meeting at a studio in Los Angeles, where I played Mario several songs from my *Green Album* and a few more I had recently written, led us to work together. We scheduled three weeks to write and record in his hometown of Detroit, Michigan.

I had barely settled into my one-bedroom, one thousand-square-foot apartment overlooking West Hollywood—backed onto the Hollywood Hills famous Runyon Canyon Park, minutes away from the famous Kodak Theatre and Hollywood Bowl—when it was time to go again.

I arrived in Toronto, where I attended business meetings with Nowack before we got into a rental car to drive to Detroit. It wasn't until we were in line to go through the Canada-U.S. border that Nowack confessed he was carrying ten thousand dollars in cash! It was a down payment Mario had demanded to produce the first song, and Nowack was having a mild panic attack that he would get caught and arrested for possessing too much cash; he panicked only because he had a fiancée now.

We drove past 8 Mile Road, made famous by rapper Eminem, the next day on our way to the studio. It was certainly a different world from what I was used to. The location was a big house, in a neighborhood of relatively small homes, with a full studio on the second floor. We were the only two white faces in the place it seemed, where everyone had a nickname (aside from Nowack and myself). Gunshots were audible from the balcony from time to time after dark, so I made sure I stayed inside. It wasn't long before we were meeting members of the famous CeCe and BeBe Winans family tree, including Vickie, Mario's mom, but this wasn't gospel we were recording.

Sessions would begin around 7:00 P.M., but Mario wouldn't arrive until at least 9:00 P.M.—finally getting creative around 11:00 P.M. It would not be unusual for us to roll out of the place between 3:00 and 4:00 A.M. Every night we waited for Mario to find his creative energy. Some nights it came; others it did not. Then the event would deteriorate into an "after party" for a bunch of unknown "friends" who would begin showing up. It was frustrating.

My daily room-to-room phone conversations with Nowack were growing increasingly impatient. I was certain it was a waste of time and money being there! Nowack wanted to believe that Mario would find his creativity and all would be saved, but I assured him, it wasn't happening. Finally Nowack, sensing it was beginning to go from bad to worse, started making phone calls.

Two weeks later, I was on a plane from Los Angeles to San Francisco, where Nowack had tracked down and arranged a meeting with legendary, multi–Grammy winning, Oscar-nominated producer, Narada Michael Walden, famous for his ten consecutive number-one hits with Whitney Houston and his work with icons such as Mariah Carey, Aretha Franklin, Sting, Stevie Wonder, and Ray Charles.

Nowack had called Narada incessantly and relentlessly until one evening he reached him at the studio. Seizing the opportunity, he pitched him everything he had on my talent and career and begged for the opportunity to meet.

And now here I was. Forty minutes into my one-on-one meeting with Narada, he was taking me from his office to his studio and placing me in front of a microphone. He looked at me and said, "This is where Whitney Houston recorded 'I Wanna Dance With Somebody' and Mariah Carey recorded 'I Don't Wanna Cry.' Now you are going to record your smash hit record."

We began recording a song I had written for charity called "I Believe"— and just like that, six hours into meeting, we were making an album together.

San Francisco!

Narada cleared his schedule to focus 100 percent on my album. A month later I was back in San Francisco, settling into my hotel, which was in a relatively new development of shops and restaurants just a few blocks away from San Quentin State Prison and the studio. I was there for a focused two and a half weeks of vocalling. It was explained to me that Narada began every track with simplicity: my vocal and a piano, keyboard, or string pad. Everything, he said, would be built up around my voice in production afterward. The most important element was my voice.

I had never worked with such a master before. He had a gift, a unique ability to evoke confidence and talent while an artist was recording. He could pull things out of your voice that you hadn't known existed! One evening after recording a beautiful ballad called "Something to Lose," Narada asked to drive me back to the hotel. During the drive, he played me the raw version of the song we had just completed. I was speechless; I had never heard myself sound like that before. It reminded me of my idols—and for a moment it seemed like time stopped and I didn't need to go any further.

We began a routine of reading a portion of Scripture before each session began. Narada would tell me to pick something that would inspire the team, give us wisdom, and lead the session. He had learned I was quite a devoted Christian, due to my refusing to work on God's day each weekend. And on one occasion it led me to call Narada (who was a Buddhist) for a ride to church, which he did, showing up in a beautiful all white suit and top hat with feather, fit for the Grammys. He went as far as to get us to sing special music for the congregation that day!

Each evening we would conclude the work by meeting at a restaurant, and most evenings, due to my dietary restrictions, I had first choice of where we would go. I introduced Narada, Nowack, and the rest of the team to all kinds of tofu, raw food, and gluten-free delicacies at which they winced and I smiled.

I traveled back and forth from Los Angeles to San Francisco every few weeks to hear how things were going; it wasn't unusual for us to go to an event or two while I was there. For example, one evening I received an invitation as we were leaving the studio. It was to a party at tennis legend Andre Agassi's house, but he wasn't the one throwing it.

The invitation had come from my friend Nick Rhodes from the 1980s band Duran Duran. I had met Nick shortly after signing with Sony Records. During my time in England, with many dinners, visits to the studio, and even recording a song together, we had developed quite a unique and strong friendship. He even referred to my mom as "Mummers." It had been a while since we had last seen each other, and it was so lovely to see a familiar face from my Sony days. There must have been 150 people at this hilltop mansion with full catering, cabanas, and any other celebrity party treat you could think of. It wasn't long before Nick and I were quietly retreating on a couch away from the party to catch up and share the latest developments of my budding career and his come back with the band. Simon, Nowack, Narada, and the rest of the guys eventually found our hideaway, and where Simon Le Bon went an entourage followed. Nowack not wanting to be outdone and most of all wanting to boast of his label talent popped one of my album demos on the system for everyone to hear. I preferred the quiet one on one conversation, but after all, it was a party.

Nowack's wedding was fast approaching in Toronto, my album was almost complete, I was dating movie stars in my downtime, and Narada and I had been asked to do a few songs together for Nowack's reception. Life was good! I went to Narada's home in Los Angeles to rehearse and contemplated sharing one particular song with him that I had just written, but I was torn. I thought perhaps I shouldn't; we were so close to being finished that I didn't want to start something new because it might mean delays with the album. But at the same time, if I waited until the next album, it might get lost in the shuffle—a second album could be years away. I sat down on the black grand piano and went for it. By the time the last note was leaving my throat, Narada was already reaching for his phone

"Nowack, Naomi just wrote a hit song. We've got to add it to the record, man."

I was excited he thought it was so good, but asked, "Should we really add it to the album? I thought we had plenty of great material."

I played it for Nowack over the phone, and the deal was done. The song was going on the album, no ifs, ands, or buts about it.

Santana in a restaurant

Two months later, we were back in San Francisco recording "Cars." It seemed that there was more excitement building over this one song than over anything else on the album! The recording session was complete and it sounded incredible. We all gathered in the lobby to decide where to eat, and I said the words everyone had been waiting to hear. It was a rather celebratory evening. Because the album was complete and this was our last end-of-production dinner together for some time, we were going to do it up, and I would go anywhere the gang wanted to eat. They voted for the finest steak house in Marin County.

I had heard people talk about it over the months, and this evening's celebration wasn't about me. I wanted to thank everyone for their hard work.

We slid into the big booth in the dimly lit restaurant. I was comfortably at the very back of the circle, fully prepared to order green beans and sautéed mushrooms when Nowack spotted someone.

"Do you see who that is?" he whispered.

"Where? The guy by himself?" I asked.

"Yes, do you see who it is?" he asked again.

"Umm . . . It could be Carlos Santana; he's wearing that beanie hat."

"It is Carlos Santana; that is him," Nowack said with a huge giddy grin.

I knew exactly what was coming. "We should invite him to join us. He's all alone."

"I don't think that is a very good idea. If he's here alone, it's because he wants to be alone, Steven," I said trying to encourage him to calm down and not embarrass the rest of us.

The next thing I knew, Nowack had the table in a huddle, crouched over the plates to announce Carlos Santana was sitting one booth over, all by himself, and he was going to invite him to join us. Narada, who had personally known Carlos for thirty-five years, quickly joined in, agreeing with me, "Calm down, don't bother him, be cool, man."

And then it happened. Nowack was excusing himself from the table and heading straight for Santana. We couldn't believe our eyes. Nowack was the opposite of subtle, and we cringed with the idea of what he was about to do and, more important, say!

He came back, returned to his seat, acting very proud of himself and calmly said,

"I just told him it was very nice to make his acquaintance and that I admired his work."

A big sigh of relief went through the group. But I knew Nowack was not finished. The wheels in his mind were saying, "I don't care what you guys think."

A few more moments went by, and then he was excusing himself again. I knew what was coming. Now was the time to duck our heads in embarrassment. Nowack went straight for Carlos once again, this time speaking with him for a few moments. Coming back toward our table, Nowack wore an ear-to-ear grin and gestured for a waiter: "We're going to need to make room for one more person to join us."

Carlos was following Nowak and carrying his plate of half-eaten steak. No one could believe their eyes. What was happening?! How had he done it? What had he said?

Carlos sat down and graciously greeted each of us. He was incredibly humble, with a peaceful spirit and quiet disposition although possessing an air that commanded absolute respect. He began to speak of his belief in God and the reason why he did what he did, saying it was all to glorify God and unify people. I sat and listened as he spoke, thinking of my goal, as we socialized for nearly three hours. Things began to noticeably wind down, and the restaurant staff was giving subtle hints they wanted to close. Not wanting to miss the opportunity, Nowack quickly switched gears of the conversation as we were slowly rising to our feet, and before I could say a word, he looked directly at Carlos and with sincerity said, "We are making an album with Narada. We actually recorded a song I think you would sound perfect on. It's called 'Cars.'"

I wanted to crawl under the table! And I was not alone. Everyone held their breath. But without hesitation, Carlos replied, "I would love to hear it; please send it to me. I will give you my contact information."

In complete and utter shock, we watched Carlos write down his home, cell, and office numbers, along with his e-mail address. Nowack had, once again, accomplished his goal.

A month later, I received a phone call from Narada as I was driving down La Cienega Boulevard in Los Angeles. "If you could have any guitar player in the world do a solo on your song, who would you choose? It can be anyone!"

I thought for a moment. I knew he was leading to something, so I didn't want to say the wrong answer. I also knew he was friends with a lot of legendary guitarists, so I began going through each of their names until I hit Santana. I was waiting for a hint, but he played it cool. "OK, I'm going to work on it. I think you're going to have someone very big playing on your song, a legend, bigger than anything."

What I didn't know was that Sony Records was in the middle of deciding whether Carlos Santana would be allowed to play guitar on "Cars." Carlos had asked them to release permission to him. He was allowed to play on only two songs per year outside of his own personal album projects—and he had requested my song, on an Indie label, be one of them.

Another month went by, and then one afternoon as I was getting out of my car at the grocery store, Nowack called and asked if I was sitting down. He had some news. "You're coming back to San Francisco in two days." He paused. "Because Carlos Santana is recording a guitar solo on your first single!"

It sounded as if Nowack was the one needing to sit down; he was ecstatic and speed-talking with excitement. Within minutes, he had filled me in on the entire story of everything that had transpired since our dinner meeting in San Francisco Bay until this very moment: the ups, the downs, the moments of great suspense, and now this. He wanted me to be as ecstatic as he was, but there simply wasn't room for someone else to express his level of excitement during the same phone conversation. I took the role as the reserved and pleased. Finally, he concluded, "It will sink in. You just have to live with what is happening! This is going to make your career!"

As I sat on the short plane ride from Los Angeles to San Francisco, I contemplated his words, and with tiny knots in my stomach, I hoped he was right.

Nowack picked me up from the airport so that there would be no delays in my arrival; this was a monumental day, and he wanted to spend every second in those next few hours vividly experiencing each moment. We arrived a little early at the studio, along with Narada, who had just pulled in with his red Mercedes convertible. The three of us met at the front door and to our surprise were greeted by Mr. Santana himself. He was early and had beat all of us to the studio! There was no entourage, manager, publicist, or handler with him; it was just Carlos and his guitar technician. We were all shocked to see a man of his stature so truly humble and down to earth.

The words I will never forget came a few hours later as I sat two feet away from Carlos in the control room. He was playing a few riffs here and there, with that signature guitar sound that you know belongs only to Santana, simply by the way the notes sing their melody. Before the track played, he turned to me and said, "I've been working on a few things, really listening to the song. You have such a beautiful voice, and the song is so strong and pure. I don't want to mess with that. I want only to enhance what you are already doing. I want to bring it to life even more. It is so powerful."

From that moment on, he referred to me as his "angel of light" who was going to revolutionize the music industry. I couldn't believe what he was saying. The track began to play, the very notes I had written quietly on my keyboard in my apartment living room, filled the studio. I had written this song not knowing what would become of it. Simply singing and playing what my heart was feeling on a lonely quiet night: wishing to give up the search for love, fearing the one who was meant for me had found someone else and I was destined to be alone. And now, in this moment, I could hear the guitar I knew so well, but it was playing the very melody I had composed. The moment was surreal. I tried to focus intently so I could remember it forever. I knew it was a moment that could define my career.

Music videos and press

The next several months were filled with anticipation. Nowack was busier than ever, scavenging for opportunities and contacts to push this release to the top. We traveled to a prestigious music festival to meet the editor of *Billboard* magazine, where I sang to him in his hotel room, and we became instant friends. He would write a feature article in *Billboard* about me and declare that I was "the commanding diva of the decade" and that my single was "the melodic debut of the year," while referring to Céline, Whitney, and Mariah in both articles and reviews.

Then we shot a music video with Santana—something none of us believed would actually happen! Nowack hired the art director from a famous traveling production called Cavalia to create a hundred-thousand-dollar music video that would be original and outstanding. It consisted of one shoot in San Francisco with Carlos for a day and one in Montreal, Canada. I felt somewhat like a bystander at the shoot with no real say in what was happening. Everyone seemed to be secretly lobbying to be in the video, even Nowack's wife and baby! I distracted myself from all of the pomp and hype by quickly falling head over heels for a man I had met hiking just a week before. Somewhere deep down I thought something had to be just about me.

It wasn't long before I was flying to Toronto to perform at celebrity charity galas, with top designer clothing lines showering their goods on me to wear. Entertainment news shows like *Entertainment Tonight* and *eTalk Daily* were jumping on board to do feature stories. Who was this Canadian girl who had been handpicked by Santana? I knew it was getting big when Lloyd Robertson, the premier nightly newscaster in Canada, ended one of his broadcasts by giving me the last five-minute feature story and in closing said, "Looks like she's on her way!"

We were in Los Angeles doing photo shoots for the album cover and artwork for ten thousand dollars with a famous team of hair, makeup, and photography that had shot dozens of celebrities. But Nowack decided the photos didn't turn out the way he wanted, so he went ahead and rented a camera, driving me to Malibu at 5:00 A.M., with no hair and makeup (other than what I had done), to shoot the album cover himself. When I received the final artwork and album booklet, I realized the project was even less about me than I had suspected when I saw that Nowack's album Thank-yous were longer than mine! I had never even seen a label owner have Thank-yous in an album before.

The trend intensified. Nowack had to control everything; he wanted to receive the glory for every detail of this project, so that when it became the "biggest thing ever," he would receive all of the praise. I was beginning to feel numb about the entire release. There was no way it could become what everyone had hoped; it was impossible for one man to be the publicist, distributor, radio liaison, manufacturer, manager, and even the mail room staff, individually mailing packages out himself.

The big release came and for a few weeks had a glimmer of shimmering hope. It debuted on the Canadian download charts at number one ahead of Black Eyed Peas, Justin Timberlake and U2 and stayed there for two or three weeks coinciding with albums selling out of stores in the first few days only to go on back-order that would never be fulfilled because a second run of the album was never ordered. Nowack was confident the heightened level of press would last forever and had no concept of how calculated and what level of planning truly went into a major label release. By the time an album hits shelves there is usually a military air-tight release, press and tour schedule to maintain a high level of interest for an extended period of time. I begged that I should be on a tour; he said No, that it was not the way he planned. I would play stadiums on my first tour and nothing else. I watched quietly as the project fizzled and burned into nothing. Pride went before the fall.

Nowack refused to give up; he refused to believe that the most valuable time an artist has is in the moments of hype from the press right before the release, and once that disappeared, it was just a moment quickly forgotten.

Two years passed, Nowack still calling every few days to say he had discovered the big thing that was going to make my career. We attended the Grammys only to watch everyone else walk by in the limelight of the success of their careers. Finally Nowack's last hurrah came when he met Archbishop Desmond Tutu in an airport lounge. In a few brief moments, he managed to convince Mr. Tutu that he was about to launch an effort of world unity: Free Music. The only thing Nowack didn't realize was that music was being shared for free already, by millions of people.

I flew to New York for the press conference for Free Music. Nowack had hired an A-list publicity firm and built the launch into a $150,000 press campaign. The venue was beautiful, the party planning was lavish, and even Larry King was there, to support his wife, who was also performing at the launch.

Desmond, Larry, his wife, and I sat backstage, waiting, but to everyone's disappointment, and my last straw, only six people from the press showed up to cover the event.

I knew I had to leave Nowack. I was scared, for many reasons. He was a man who never accepted the word No, and I was sure he simply wouldn't let me leave. I also had no financial security. I had been very tightly guarded, not being allowed to earn additional income through touring and shows. When I tried to get into an alternative career in acting, Nowack called the producer of my first audition and killed it. No one had wanted to work with me because of it. I had also been convinced that at my age of twenty-six, he was the only person willing to work with me.

I couldn't understand how God had not rescued the situation. I had been given every opportunity to succeed—a second time—and He had not intervened to bring it to success. I began to again despise my gift of singing. Why had God given me the talent if He refused to help me become a success with it? I was teaching Bible classes every week at church. I was one of the leaders for community outreach, leading church groups to places such as the Santa Monica pier, where we gave away bottles of water to passers-by, along with verses about the "true living water." I was even a church board member! My heart had been broken with failed, temporary relationships. It didn't seem that God was with me at all; I just felt like giving up.

In my wish to escape, I decided to volunteer for a mission trip to Honduras. Church members donated the funds for me, and I went for ten days. It was a wonderful feeling to be away from the pressure of Hollywood and my career.

New York hip-hop studio calling

I received a phone call from Mario Winans in New York. He was working closely with Puff Daddy in his downtown studio and had a concept for us to work on together. I hadn't really spoken to him since Detroit. I was excited but at the same time hesitant because of how things had turned out the first time. Simply out of desperation and the need to feel like I was still "in the business," I agreed.

Upon landing in New York, the questions only intensified. What was I doing? Why was I here? Was this what I had come to? I pleaded with God to give me a break. I couldn't go back to playing in bookstores again, and I simply didn't have any other talents to begin a new career.

Chapter 11
At the Crossroads

Upon landing in New York City, I received a text message from Mario asking if I would join him and some business partners he wanted me to meet for dinner. It was 5:15 P.M., and I was asked to come straight to the studio.

I arrived at "Daddy's House" (named after Sean "Puff Daddy" Combs) in midtown around 6:00 P.M. It was a dark studio with seemingly black walls and metal fixtures. The décor was minimal, masculine, and not very inviting, with two huge industrial doors leading to a no-nonsense receptionist. Once inside there was a hallway that led to more hallways and doors that led to secondary doors with small round peep holes that would bring you into each studio's control room. It seemed very secretive, perhaps in case any wannabes wandered in. Big bodyguards and hip-hop producers were behind most of the doors while a chef hung out in the kitchen, but no matter what he was cooking, the smell of marijuana wafted through the hallway.

We finally left for dinner at around 9:00 P.M. Mario, a group of guys from the studio, and I piled into one big, black, bulletproof, SUV with a chauffeur (or "driver" as they called him).

I was hesitant from the moment I stepped off the plane. I knew coming on this trip would be a compromise to what I really wanted for my career, which was to be a strong solo female vocalist. I was there to discuss a rock/hip-hop band with me as the front woman. At this point, I was so broken from my failures that I was willing to grasp at straws, hoping for one last break that would prove I wasn't a failure. *God had obviously turned a blind eye to my career,* I rationalized, *so maybe it is time I start following all of the opportunities presented to me—even if they don't feel 100 percent appropriate. Who knows how many opportunities I have turned down in the past that could have propelled my career,* I reasoned.

We arrived at a swanky restaurant in the meatpacking district of Manhattan, and I soon realized my idea of a dinner meeting was wildly out of sync with a hip-hop dinner meeting. We didn't leave the restaurant until midnight, and by then there must have been twenty additional people with us. I was anxious to talk business and hear of this great plan, but the subject didn't come up. Not tonight, I was told. It was time to have fun and celebrate!

My luggage was in the back of the big SUV, which more or less meant I was stuck with the group, until I could be driven to my hotel room to check in. If I departed now, whatever deal was pending might never happen. The next stop was the club. Everyone piled out and headed to the VIP line. I hesitated; I noticed the chauffer was staying in the vehicle. I asked Mario if he was coming: "Nah, this ain't his thing. He's religious."

An overwhelming wave of guilt washed through me. *I'm religious. It isn't my thing either.* But there I was, following the crowd of hip-hoppers into a club. The feeling remained. *What am I doing here?*

At 3:30 A.M., I finally crawled into bed, disgusted and wishing to forget about the entire evening of what seemed like nonstop and out-of-control chaos that brought me to what felt like the devil's den. My hair and clothes reeked of smoke, pot, and alcohol. *What a hypocrite,* I thought, while the feeling of shame washed over me.

I had always been the one who was strongly convicted. I was the one who set the example. But not that night. I was just like everyone else—a follower. So what if I had never drank a sip of alcohol in my life or touched a cigarette or experimented with drugs? How would anyone know that who saw me in that dark hip-hop club? I kept thinking, *What if Jesus had come in that very moment?* But I rationalized, *He still would save me; I just know it.*

The next morning came. I was in no rush; I had most of the day to contemplate my life and career before I was expected at the studio. And I did just that, feeling lost with no vision and confused with my future prospects.

I entered the studio determined to hear the plan. I wasn't going to waste more time or ride another party train around town. I walked in to find Mario getting his hair cut by a barber, yes right there in the control room with several people hanging out, jamming to various sample tracks.

"We're going to go to dinner in a bit. You're coming with us, right?" Mario said.

"Uh . . . yeah, I guess so," was my response.

I was thinking, *No, no, no,* but those other words came out anyway. The air was thick with smoke so I stepped into the hallway. It was Friday evening, the sun was hanging low, it was 5:30 P.M., and soon it would be dark. I didn't want to be there; the last thing I wanted was a repeat of the previous night—and I knew it would be just that. The best compromise was to speak privately about business, but even that was something I didn't want to do after the sun had set. I began to pace the long, narrow hallway. I almost made it to the exit but turned back. *I can't just leave,* I thought. *I have to let Mario know where I am going, and I'd have to say why I am leaving.* But I'd already said Yes. My mind was screaming at me to make a decision. It would have been so easy if I had stood my ground the night before.

As I stood in the center of the hallway, I realized how quiet it had become, like no one else was there, until I noticed the chauffer approaching me. He was wearing his signature knee-high white socks, jeans shorts, and team jersey. I smiled politely as he drew closer and said, "Hi. How are you?" as a courtesy, expecting him to pass by. I was a bit surprised when he stopped directly in front of me. I backed into the wall to make more room for him to pass, but he did not. Instead, he looked directly into my eyes and began to speak very seriously.

"I had a dream about you last night."

I was shocked! His statement was wildly inappropriate! Even if he had had a dream, he never should have mentioned it. But before responding, I quickly weighed the consequences of telling him so. He was responsible for driving me to and from the studio and eventually back to the airport, so I should be nice. In addition, he was supposedly a Christian.

"Oh really, what was it about?" I asked.

"An angel came to me in the night and told me he had a message for me to tell you," he continued.

It was the furthest thing from what I had expected him to say. I honestly had no idea what to expect, but it wasn't that! I was curious to know more; after all, it is very unusual for someone to have an angel visit them in a dream with a message. But I wanted to keep things light at the same time. I didn't know who this guy was but assumed that he might be a street preacher in his spare time.

"What did the angel say?" I asked.

"The words I am about to say to you are not mine; they were given to me by the Holy Spirit," he replied.

I now froze in place.

"You think that you can live your life doing whatever you want, jumping from side to side when you feel like it. Being a good Christian girl, teaching Bible classes, attending church regularly, looking like a saint to all the people who know you. But then you jump to the other side to a place where those church people wouldn't recognize you—going in the club, associating with people who are filled with darkness, doing things you shouldn't do, living however you want to live. You think there are no consequences. You think you are so clever playing both sides, like you'll never get caught. But one day, when it's too late, you will get caught, caught on the wrong side, wishing you had made a decision, and one day it will be too late to make a decision."

He was standing so close to me that I could feel his breath. I knew what he was saying was true, but my doubting heart believed he must have learned it somewhere from someone. My mind raced as he spoke. *Who told him this? Where did he read this? Is this on the Internet somewhere?* The knots were forming in my stomach as my entire body tensed.

"You keep asking, 'Why?' " he continued. "You keep asking why this keeps happening to you. Why, every time you are given a rare opportunity to succeed and everything is laid out in front of you as though you are climbing to the top of the mountain, ready to reach out and grab a hold of your every dream you have ever had coming true, it crumbles into dust at your feet. And it keeps happening to you! Over and over again. And you want to know why. And whether it will happen again. And whether it will continue to happen."

Tears were filling my eyes. Every word he spoke was implanted in my heart; they were the very words I had spoken in conversation with God as I pleaded for an answer to what seemed like a never-ending question of "Why?" They were my prayers. My agony and despair. And only God had heard them; only He had known these words.

"The answer is Yes, it will happen again; Yes, it will continue to happen. This cycle will never be broken; it will never stop. Unless you make a decision here and now. You are at a crossroads today. There are two paths for you to choose between. One will lead you further into what you already know. You will chase after what you want, what you think you want, and everything you think will make you happy. And it will lead you back to the same place you are now, asking 'Why?' With a pile of dust at your feet.

"Or you can choose a new path, one where you give up all that you want, everything you think you need, and stop chasing after your own desires, one where you give it all to God and let Him lead. Only then will the cycle stop. Only then will you get everything you've ever wanted. Only then will your dreams come true."

My entire body was shaking. I knew without a shadow of a doubt that God had just used this man to speak to me. I feared I was going to burst into tears; and I had to get out of there. The only words I could muster were, "Thank you," as I began to walk toward the exit. "I have to go," I said as my walk turned into a run through the doors, down the stairs, and onto the street. My mind was reeling. I was panic-stricken and humbled all at the same time as I tried to hold back the shock and emotions from bursting out of me. I wanted to scream out on the street, "God just spoke to me!" but I knew no one would understand. I hailed a cab and told the cab driver to take me to my hotel. The only two people I thought might even partially understand were my parents. I called them right away. I didn't know what to say as I tried to find coherent words that made sense. I tried to tone it down so as not to alarm them and felt as though I would burst if I didn't share it with someone.

I stepped into my hotel room and could not hold back the emotion any longer. The tears and heart-wrenching sobs began to flow as I knelt down beside my bed and began to pray. "God, I can't believe You did that for me, that I would be worth so much that You would send me a direct message through someone, to reach me. Thank You, God, thank You."

God had heard my prayers all along.

Chapter 12
America's Idol

It wasn't difficult for me to return to California. The truth is that business was never directly spoken about during the days I spent in New York on that trip.

When I got to back to Los Angeles, I still felt that I didn't know what to do or which direction to take. I knew God was with me and had heard my cry, but I but didn't know what that meant for my immediate future. My finances were about to completely dry up as I officially dissolved my partnership with Nowack. One thing was certain: Los Angeles had changed for me. It was no longer a beautiful, fun, inspiring location to live. It was as if the curtain had been pulled back, allowing me to see everything and everyone for who and what they really were—and it was frightening. The self-love was overwhelming, and the shallow interactions became repulsive. I kept asking myself, *Where is God in all of this?* I could tell I was changing, but I still didn't know what direction to take.

Once I had ended my partnership with Nowack, I knew I could not continue paying $1,650 in rent each month. I took a temp job for a church member filing health-clinic paperwork, but that job didn't pay enough to sustain my lifestyle. I knew that it was time I got out of Los Angeles.

Instead of letting go of my amazing apartment, someone suggested that I sublet it for a few months while I was away, figuring out what I would do next. That sounded like a great idea, and many people I knew had done it successfully. I posted an online ad, and within a day or two I had a response—a woman with a child.

Soon I was back in Ontario, Canada, back in the room where I had retreated during my first career disappointment, but this time I was not depressed. I was simply waiting for the next step, for God to send me a new direction.

During the first two months of being home, I was contacted with a surprising request—to be a speaker at the very camp I had attended as a youth. The invitation was intriguing because I had never done anything like it. I was also able to broker a deal for my *Green Album* with the help of my dad. It was going to be purchased from a woman I had become friends with in Los Angeles. She was a music licensor for films and TV shows, and she wanted to buy the half of the album from me and become a co-owner. It was a huge blessing.

However, while that purchase was taking place, another enormous problem was developing. My tenant's first and second months' rent checks had bounced; it was quickly becoming obvious that she was not who she claimed to be. Christmas was fast approaching, and Mom was warning me that my present might be an empty apartment when I returned to Los Angeles. The lease had been for six months, but after just two months, it was clear the sublet arrangement wouldn't work.

I received a phone call January 1 that something terrible had happened. The six months' worth of post-dated checks the woman had given me, plus a cleaning deposit check—which I had placed in the care of a financial manager in Los Angeles—had *all* been accidentally deposited by a new account manager, who had failed to check the dates. It meant that literally thousands of dollars would be bouncing. When I attempted to phone the woman, she was nowhere to be found. Those facts meant that I needed to return to Los Angeles immediately.

I booked a flight with the cheapest airfare flying out of Toronto. It was an unlikely flight for me to be on because it had me flying east to Philadelphia before heading to the West Coast, and out of two options I had, it was unusual that I had chosen that particular flight. The next day my parents drove me to the airport and wished me well. The only bright side was that the album sale was on the verge of being finalized. It was the blessing that kept me from becoming discouraged.

While in Philadelphia waiting for my connecting flight, I heard an announcement for my flight. The airline had overbooked and needed a volunteer to give up his or her seat and take the following flight. In exchange for a few-hours' delay, they would reward that person with a free flight voucher. I jumped at the opportunity and rushed to the gate. I was in no hurry to get back to whatever awaited me at my apartment, and a free flight could come in handy! I was first in line and was told to wait until the flight had been fully seated before coming to collect my voucher. I sat back down, opened a book, and began to read to pass the time.

"Would Naomi Striemer please come to gate twenty-seven," came over the louder speaker. *That's me! Time to pick up my free voucher,* I thought. "It turns out there is one seat left on the plane, miss. It is in first class. We are going to give you this seat *and* give you the free flight voucher for being willing to volunteer."

I was overjoyed. I thanked God for this little blessing that lifted my spirits and gave me the courage I needed to tackle any difficulty ahead.

I had never sat in first class before, so I was excited. Because I was the last person to board, all eyes were on me as I strolled in and lifted my carry-on for storage above my seat. Upon doing so, I looked around and realized that Randy Jackson, from *American Idol,* was sitting directly behind me! Immediately I thought, *Randy will never recognize me,* but my mom's words were ringing in my ears: *"Stop thinking that you are invisible when you see people you know!"* When I mustered up the courage to say Hi, the word had barely escaped my lips before Randy was jumping up from his seat to give me a big hug.

"Naomi, dawg, how have you been! This is wild, man, this is wild."

I was overtaken by his response. "Dude, this is Naomi Striemer. She is an amazing singer!" he declared to the entire first-class section. "She sings one of my favorite songs, what's it called? 'Something to Lose'— that's it!" as he broke into the chorus of the song!

I was stunned! *Is this really happening?* I felt as though I had just stepped into a crazy dream sequence. I wasn't even supposed to be in first class, let alone on this flight! *How was this happening? And what were the chances?* It lifted me to cloud nine. Life suddenly didn't seem so dreary after all. Prayers of thanks and amazement were leaving my mind almost faster than I could think them.

As we taxied to the runway, Randy and I continued in conversation.

He wanted to know everything that had happened since we last met and how things had ended between Nowack and me. Another passenger had graciously traded seats so that Randy and I could visit, and during the seat shuffle Randy introduced me to another celebrity in first class, one of his friends, Oscar-winning actor Terrence Howard, who had also recorded an album.

For the next five hours, Randy, Terrence, and I visited about music, songs, artists, plans, and the future all while periodically passing our iPods to one another to hear certain songs and collaborations we had individually worked on. By the time the flight landed, I had made a new friend, and Randy had given me his contact information to get in touch with him for a meeting at his office. He had a project in mind, and I was just the girl he had wanted to see about it. Terrence had also given me his contact numbers because, he said, we were destined to write a song together.

It was the most enjoyable plane ride of my life. God must have known I could not have handled the demolished state of my apartment if it had not been for that incredible once-in-a-lifetime flight.

I turned the key and walked into what looked like a scene from a drug-bust movie. Blood, vomit, and other stains were on all of the walls, carpet, and flooring. Every piece of furniture had been moved and rearranged to resemble a red-light district one only reads about. All of my beautiful paintings, artifacts, and sculptures had been put away in drawers and closets. The microwave had been brought into the living room to sit beside the couch in front of the TV. The blinds were all drawn, and the toilets were not flushed. Pieces of needles were strewn in the corners. I couldn't imagine the horror that had taken place in my beloved apartment in two months to create this condition. If the apartment had instead been a solitary house in an open space, I would have lit a match and burned the place down. It reeked of sin and sadness. Never would I have imagined this was possible from the clean-cut, dignified woman who had applied for the lease with her five-year-old daughter at her side.

Thankfully, with hard work, rubber gloves, and a tough stomach, almost any cleanup is possible! And within three days memories of what my apartment once resembled were coming back as I took out bag after bag of garbage and broken items. It was a life lesson learned.

Henson Studios

I borrowed a friend's little old blue Toyota Tacoma and learned how to drive stick shift, which in Los Angeles is tricky! There seemed to be a hill at every turn. One of my first destinations was Randy Jackson's office, located at the very prestigious Henson Studios located only two blocks down the hill from my apartment. I coasted down to the security gate to announce my appointment. Cringing at what the security guard must be thinking, which I was sure included some sort of, "Yea right, lady; there's no way you have an appointment," I smiled as my name was confirmed from inside the studio. My smile quickly faded back to embarrassment as I stalled the truck halfway through the gate heading to the parking lot.

I found my way to Randy's office through the big complex of buildings after being directed at reception in the main studio. It was the kind of place where you saw famous people while just waiting for your own meeting, and I did, with a few band leaders passing by and saying "Hello."

Randy was situated in a cottagelike office section just above the VIP parking, where his Bentley was parked beside several Mercedes and Jaguars. I was greeted by his friendly assistant. We had spoken on the phone, and she had been expecting me. She led me through the fashionable reception area of his office where his two assistants worked and into the kitchen/snack area, where Randy was waiting. The room was warm and fun with delectable treats in big glass jars and baskets with healthy sodas in packs next to a mini fridge. It was everything you could imagine putting in a studio/office snack room. No expense had been spared. The colors were bright, and the sun shone through the window at the end of room. Randy got up with a friendly smile to give me a big hug and then invited me to sit down. "Let's talk!" he said. He was such a happy person, and his office and staff reflected his personality. It seemed like a breath of fresh air from what I had been doing for the previous few days.

After a half hour of small talk, Randy presented his concept to me. He wanted to put together a "superband" as he put it. It would consist of a few ladies and a few gentlemen who were all talented enough to be solo artists and could all play instruments. He said there was nothing like it, and it would be perfect for the market! And he wanted to start with me as the first member. I was instantly deflated. A superband was not what I had in mind. I felt as though I was fifteen years old again at TransCon studios saying that I didn't want to be in a group; I wanted to be a solo artist. But then the voice in my head reminded me that the opportunities I had taken had not panned out. Perhaps I should stop being so picky! I hesitated and asked a lot of questions. It seemed Randy was doing a very good job at convincing me it was a great idea. I agreed to see how it went for a few weeks as he introduced me to a few possible band mates. It wasn't what I had hoped for, but Randy was one of the biggest names in pop culture and had an unlimited budget. Maybe it could turn into something.

As the sale of my *Green Album* was finalizing, I was being introduced to future band mate number one, whom I will call Tina, a young, round-faced, curly haired Jewish girl in her early twenties, who rarely went anywhere without her guitar. She had a hippie type of personality and was fairly new to the business. She had grown up in the valley as the child of a famous band member. She was sweet and kind of shy— but only on the surface. We wrote a song on my couch within a few hours of meeting each other, recorded it on a cell phone, and e-mailed it to Randy. He was on the phone within minutes. "That's da bomb! You girls just wrote a hit song! Keep writing more. Yeah, yeah." *Maybe there is something to this band idea after all,* I told myself.

The next day I was introduced to a girl Tina wanted to bring into the band. I will call her Aubree. They had met only days earlier at a famous clothing designer's dinner party. Aubree was a former child movie star who had ended up on Broadway and had gone off the tracks. She was now pursuing a career in music, her first love, and was currently clean. She, too, was a Jewish girl who had grown up in the valley but had a much spunkier personality than Tina and was not afraid to share her opinion—and didn't bother to state it politely. I could tell these two girls were going to bond in a way that I would not be able to, but I pushed past those thoughts to what might come from this opportunity.

Once again, within hours of meeting each other, Aubree and I had written an amazing song, and once again Randy was on the phone saying he was very excited about the prospects of what was happening with us three girls.

We continued to get together and have writing sessions, and the songs continued to flow; there was no denying the songs had magic. We were a good writing combination, although it was becoming more apparent I was the odd girl out. Our lifestyles, upbringings, and beliefs were vastly different. I simply couldn't relate when both would converse about "going clean" or what it was like at their "rock bottom"; and when we would go grab a bite to eat, both would agonize over weight issues—something I had never struggled with, due to my rigorous dietary restriction. I tried my best to sympathize and create similarities that could be viewed as relatable, but it was obvious that as the two girls grew closer, I was pushed further away.

Randy wanted us to continue looking for male band members, but it seemed as though the task was impossible. We met with a few guys he liked, but we all agreed it wasn't a good "flow"; then the girls brought in other guys they knew, including a young man named Reeve Carney. He was tall, thin, a bit odd—but had captivating personality. He dressed like an 1800s Civil War pirate. He was a good Christian boy and wildly talented, seemingly the perfect fit! Until he politely and quietly told us that he was already in a band signed to Universal Records. Little did we know he would go on to star in Broadway's *Spiderman* and become a big star.

Finding a name for our group was becoming just as challenging as finding male band members. We went through hundreds of options, but none seemed to fit; and if they did, the three of us could never agree; and in the off-chance we did, Randy would say the name wasn't right for us.

As time passed the girls' bond began to control the group. I was being left out of details and overall felt confused as to why I was even in the group. Then I would remind myself of how wonderful Randy was, and I'd continue on. Quickly we had written nearly twenty songs, and they were great songs, quite possibly hit songs; no one could deny it.

Meanwhile, I was living on the money I had earned from the sale of my album, but that wouldn't last forever. If something didn't take place soon, I would be back in the same situation as before. At this time I began attending a nightly series of religious meetings held by my favorite evangelist, Pastor Shawn Boonstra. I had watched his entire series of DVDs and was certainly not going to miss hearing him live, regardless of what plans the girls had. Every evening I would attend the meetings, and every night I would leave the meetings feeling re-vitalized. Seeing familiar Christian friends and making new ones was becoming more and more important. I was not with my kind of people during the day when I would work with the girls. We had different goals. I remembered what I had set out to do when I was a teenager, which was to witness through music, but I couldn't do that with this group. No wonder it was not working. I needed to be with people who believed like I did, who believed in the power of God! I kept asking myself, *What am I doing wasting my time, when our time on this earth is so precious and so fleeting?*

As my convictions began to grow, it seemed turmoil within the group followed. It was no longer a secret that the girls wanted me out. The culminating event was a trip to Las Vegas to see the girls' favorite band of all time—the Dave Matthews Band—whom they idolized. I declined to participate in the trip. I wasn't going to get stuck in Las Vegas, a place I already disliked immensely, in a hotel room provided by the trumpet player of the Dave Matthews Band to be a groupie hang-ing out backstage and partying all weekend. It sounded like a night-mare, and was certainly not the situation I wanted to put myself in. My decision did not go over well, to say the least. Whatever fury they had been holding back came out in full force, and I got an earful on their way out of town. My convictions would cause my separation from this band, I was told, as they hung up the phone.

We were only weeks away from signing a lucrative deal with Sony Publishing, something I had wanted my entire career. It would be the first money we would see as a group, and Randy had put it together for us since his deal with us had not included a financial advance. It seemed the business was coming together for our little nameless group, regardless of the behind-the-scenes disagreements. Finally, we went to the studio to record our first song together, passing Mick Jagger and Joss Stone on the way into Studio A, the biggest room Henson Studios had. After hours of recording, it just didn't seem to be clicking the way it should, and the recording was a flop.

A few days later, I received a text from the girls to meet at Tina's apartment to rehearse; little did I know it was an ambush. But I knew something was wrong the moment I came in; the tension in the air could have been cut with a knife, and the girls both sat stiffly on the couch. I sat on the solo chair nearby and asked what was going on.

Never in my life had I ever experienced venom spewing out of someone's mouth the way that it happened in those next few moments. The girls had fully prepared what they would say. They felt as though my Christianity was a hindrance to the band and that I was going to hold them back. "How can we move forward if you don't believe in this one hundred percent? *Nothing* can be more important to you than this band!" they demanded.

I came back with the truth. "God is the most important thing in my life, and whatever I do on this earth will never be more important than my relationship with God."

It was as if the two girls were no longer in their own bodies. I knew I was no longer speaking to Tina or Aubree, but to the devil himself. The words reminded me so closely of the conversation the serpent had with Eve in the Garden.

"This band is here and now. God can wait! What kind of a God wouldn't want you following your dreams?" came their slippery reply. "He doesn't sound like a great God to me!"

"At the end of the day, I want to have a relationship with my Savior, the One who made me, so I can spend eternity with Him. Not a few moments of empty glory here on this earth. Nothing can compare to that! Certainly not a few fleeting moments of fame! I'm not giving up my conviction or beliefs for that or anything else."

As I spoke and listened, I continued in prayer for God to protect me and give me the right words to say. I knew this was a battle far bigger than our band, and it was clearer than ever what I had to do.

"You have expressed how you feel, and it is only fair that I remove myself from the band so that you can pursue your path without my hindrance any longer. I know what I want in life, and it's not this!" I said as I got up to leave.

The girls were frantic and beside themselves with anger and frustration.

"You can't just leave! We have to tell Randy."

"I will be glad to call Randy and tell him," I promised.

On my way back to my apartment, I called Randy and told him that I was quitting the band. Nothing would step between my God and me.

In his typical no-stress demeanor, Randy tried to convince me everything could be worked out, it must not be as bad as it sounded or seemed. He asked if he could get the other two girls together with me for a lunch the following day. I agreed.

Randy knew how strongly committed I was to my beliefs. We had conversed for many hours in the studio regarding my lifestyle. He had shared his past and why he had stepped away from the church, and I had pointed out how it's never too late to come back. People, not God, ruin Christianity's reputation, I had said.

For weeks my mind had been brought back to the conversation I had had with the chauffeur in the hip-hop studio in New York. God had put him there for a reason. It was a message I was not to take lightly—but now here I was following my original dream once again. I felt it more and more. I didn't want to be a part of the world. I wanted to be a light shining to make a difference.

We met the next day for lunch at Randy's favorite restaurant, a beautiful picturesque celebrity hangout. Randy jokingly said he felt like Pontius Pilate sitting as the judge in this situation. In his irony there was great truth. Randy and I listened as Tina and Aubree expressed their case; their perception of my faith being a hindrance to the groups' progress was the main concern.

"Can't you be more flexible about the situation?" Randy asked me.

"When you're on tour with the girls, you stay as a group and do every-thing as a group? And then when you are home away from the group, you do as you please with your religious convictions?"

I saw that he simply did not understand. My faith was not a turn-on, turn-off option. "I am who I am and I believe strongly. I am not willing to change and be a part-time Christian to accommodate the group," I responded. "I'm sorry."

"Well isn't this ironic?" Randy said. "We have two Jews and a Chris-tian fighting over a Sabbath issue. The only thing is, the Christian is fighting for the Sabbath, and the Jews are fighting against it!"

No truer words were ever spoken.

We left with no solution in sight. I phoned Randy as I drove home and told him it was the end. There was nothing he could do that would make me stay with the group. I had to pursue what was in my heart—and that was to follow Christ's path for me. I had to discover what His plan for my life was, and I had to serve Him fully.

Randy listened until the end of my statement before speaking. And then he said something I will never forget: "Now that you have made this decision, I can't ask you to stay; I can't force you to stay because I can't put you on stage to sing these songs in front of an audience. They will never believe you because they will sense that you don't believe what you are singing—that you are faking it. Your truth is singing for Jesus now. The only thing you can do now is go sing for Jesus. You have my full support."

And just like that it hit me. Why had I been wasting my time? I was supposed to sing for Jesus! The reason He had given me this talent in the first place was to do just that, and I had been squandering it, chasing after my own dreams and for what—a pile of dust at my feet!

Chapter 13
My Incomparable God

I was terrified but overjoyed at the same time. I had never felt so strong and so confident than at this very moment. I knew God was in control. Finally, I could stop pushing so hard for everything I had thought I wanted. I could relax in the arms of Jesus and wait upon His plan. I knew I was free-falling and was about to run out of money, but I didn't care. The chains had been broken; I was indeed a free woman. I had made a stand for Jesus and I was exultant. Although the world would never understand, I knew I had won the victory. Never again would I turn back to chase after this world.

For years leading up to this moment, every time I opened my Bible it would land in one particular spot, and my eyes would focus on the same verse that I had underlined years before: "What shall it profit a man, if he shall gain the whole world, and lose his own soul? Or what shall a man give in exchange for his soul?" (Mark 8:36, 37, KJV).

So many times I had looked at that verse wondering why my Bible always opened to that same spot. It had always touched deep into my soul, those profound words. Yet every time I read it, and every time I was touched by it, I never felt as though I was the one losing my soul to gain the world. Perhaps there were moments I felt I could have corrected a single decision or two in the recent weeks or days leading up to seeing that verse again, but never did I have the overwhelming sense that every day that I was choosing a path that was for my own selfish gain, to place me and my talent and my accomplishments high on a pedestal for the world to see and admire, I was forfeiting my soul. With every decision that I made for myself and not for God's glory, I was guilty of this exchange. I was making the choice that my will and my decisions were more important. But now I realized that one is either "with" or "against" God's will, and for every moment that God was not being actively lifted up and glorified was a moment I was losing my soul.

There were many who openly disagreed with my decision, calling me dumb, stupid, or even arrogant to think I would be better off without this opportunity. Both extended family and friends tried to coax me into "wiser" thinking, to go back and mend the situation. "Surely it couldn't have been that bad," I was told.

But I would never look back. I would never regret my decision. It was the day that had set me free. I had been given a new life and felt as though I could live with any decision God felt was right for me. Joy had entered my soul, and I could see a new day dawning on the horizon. My parents stood strongly by my side and reassured me everything would work out.

Welcome to camp

I was three weeks away from flying to Nova Scotia to be the youth speaker at the very camp I had grown up attending. I had almost forgotten the appointment during the ordeal I had experienced in the previous six months.

Now I began to be filled with renewed energy and joy at the thought that I was being asked to speak and preach to youth for an entire week! And, oh, did I have a message to share with them! I had never before been asked to be a youth speaker and had preached in church only once. But I knew that with God's help, I was fully capable of the task at hand. Secretly, I had admired evangelists, including my own father, from a very young age and had listened intently as they gave seminars and series of meetings. Through my years of teaching Bible classes, I had harbored a deep desire to one day have the honor of being asked to speak in such a way. God was already beginning to answer my prayers to reveal a plan He had laid out for me.

I carefully began crafting eleven sermons to share with the young people my story and my testimony; I wanted to shout from the rooftops, "Jesus saves! And He can save you too!" I wanted to explain that I had seen many of the great things of the world people clamor after, and they are nothing when compared to Jesus' great gift to us at the cross. If I could convict only one soul against chasing after the long, tiring, and destructive path this world has to offer, I would feel my journey of disappointment and heartbreak would all be worth it.

It was as if a light began to shine brightly on each story and it brought to mind moments that at the time seemed insignificant but now appeared to be defining moments in my life and journey, turning points that I had been unaware of. I began to see the true nature of what had been taking place and glimpse divine intervention in the great controversy that rages over each and every one of us. Questions I had held unanswered for many years seemed to be inspiring answers, and I began to realize that in the moments I thought God had disserted me, it had been the complete opposite. He had stepped in to prepare a way for this very moment to happen. Every failed attempt at success now began to appear as part of the divine plan to draw me closer to God, and more and more I began to realize how intimately God had been with me through it all.

I stepped on a plane with my sermons tucked in my laptop bag. I knew I probably wouldn't be meeting any celebrities on this flight, and even if I did, they would never be able to deter me from my mission. I was headed back to the place where it had all begun; the place where life had been simple and wholesome, before I had discovered the busy alluring world and all it had to offer with its smoke and mirrors. The place where a young girl once believed the Bible was still being written. It seemed my life was coming back around full circle, and I was returning as the person I had dreamt of becoming when I was that little girl, a person who could lead great multitudes to Christ Jesus.

My parents decided to take the eighteen-hour drive from Ontario to Nova Scotia to meet me upon my arrival at the camp. It would be a thirteen-year reunion for each of us to step foot onto that beach-front camp property with cabins facing the long and sandy beach on the north shore where you could watch the sun rise for miles.

My parents arrived mere moments before I was dropped off in front of the little white cabin that was first in line on Speakers' Row. I immediately realized that this achievement, small by the world's standards, meant more to me than all of the newspaper pages I had once graced. I was at this camp as an official ambassador for God. My parents and I embraced with joy and gratitude and stood in silence listening to the ocean lap up on the shore, allowing the magnitude of the situation to sink in.

I walked the short distance to the big youth tent the next evening to begin my meetings, and with great joy I began to share my stories. Each evening it seemed more and more faces would appear in the tent, young and old alike. I was being filled with gratitude and a sense of awe, experiencing the hand of God at work.

Little did I know that God had the biggest gift of my life waiting for me during this very week. Months earlier, I become utterly discouraged that I would never meet a suitable husband. My many dating experiences through the years had all ended in heartbreak and disappointment. My expectations were too great and my list of requirements was too long. Now I decided to give my desire for a Christian husband to God. I had read that being specific in prayer was important. On the list I had gone for a practical "kind heart" and a fantasy "blond and blue eyes" and a downright picky "vegetarian" who "doesn't drink," "believes like I do," and then who is fun and "adventurous" and finally "loves to laugh."

I had concluded by saying, "Dear God, if it's meant to be, please find me a husband. I would like to be married one day in the not-too-distant future. After all, I am twenty-six, and I made a declaration at an early age that I would be married at twenty-seven. I can't seem to find anyone on my own."

On Tuesday afternoon, I was walking back to my cabin from the cafeteria and was stopped by a concerned father. He had been in my meetings every evening and was enjoying them thoroughly. His son was arriving that very day, and he wanted him to also attend my meetings—and perhaps even to meet me. I envisioned a sixteen-year-old, pimply faced boy, and said, "Of course." At that precise moment, the father stated, "Well wouldn't you know it; here he comes now!" I turned around to meet this young lad only to realize he was not a teenager! He was a tall, blond, blue-eyed adult man who had just returned from a mountain biking trip.

Yes . . . he was the man I was going to marry.

All those years and all of that time, God had been waiting for me to come around and to choose His plan for my life, the perfect plan, the one He had designed before I was even born, and I had been so stubborn for so long. Oh, if we could only see the life God has planned for us. He is waiting for each and every one of us in the same way He waited for me. Our plans are so small and broken compared to His.

I could tell you that since then life has never been difficult again and I never faced another struggle—but that would be unrealistic. Life will always have challenges, but I can truly state that the bumps along the way are totally different when all things in life have been released to God's care, and all efforts are focused on praising, honoring, and sharing the love of God with others. When plans change now, I see the hand of God at work, and I know He is the One in charge, guiding and leading my life. If a door closes, I know He will open a better one. How can I be anything but absolutely content with wherever His plan leads me; after all He wants the best for me in this life, and I remember what He has done for me in the past, every little miracle that brought me to this point.

I knew without a shadow of a doubt during that week of affirmation that God was guiding my every step and I would never have to doubt or fear or become brokenhearted again. He is the same God yesterday, today, and tomorrow, and He would never let me down. And He never has.

Photo Gallery

⇧ Stiking a pose at two years old!

⇨ Apple picking.

⇩ Family portrait on the farm—with Nathan, Mom, and Dad holding me.

⇧ Holding our new bunny rabbits—with Nathan.
⇩ Watching a lamb being born—with Nathan and Dad.

⇧ Feeding the goats—with Nathan and Dad.
⇩ In my favorite place, the barn—with Nathan.

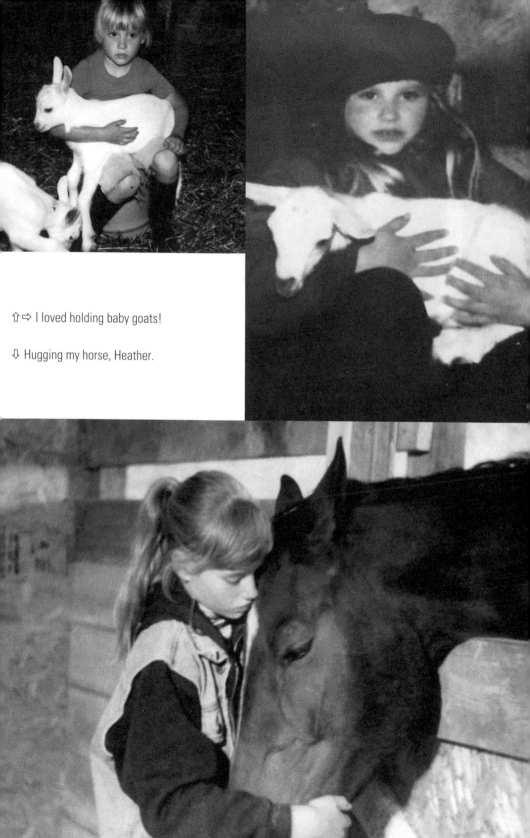

⇧ ⇨ I loved holding baby goats!

⇩ Hugging my horse, Heather.

⇦ One of my church performances
  —with Dad on guitar.

⇩ Practicing my typing skills
  —with Dad.

⇧ Shots from the $22.5k album photo shoot!

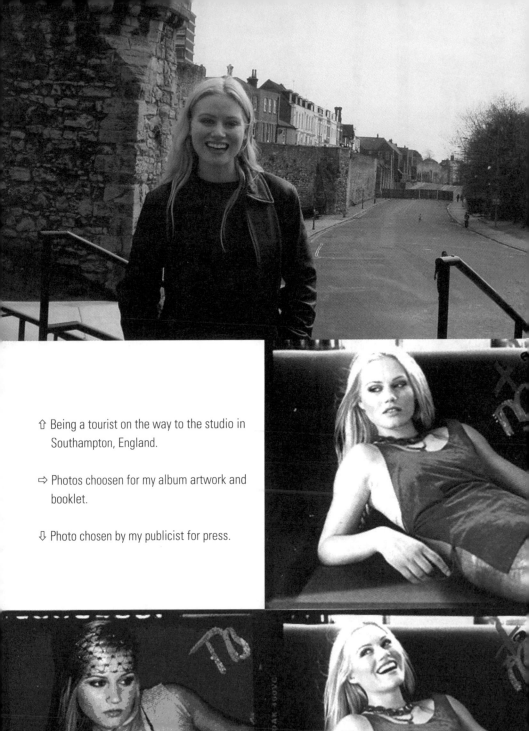

⇧ Being a tourist on the way to the studio in Southampton, England.

⇨ Photos choosen for my album artwork and booklet.

⇩ Photo chosen by my publicist for press.

⇧ A very proud moment with the orchestra recording my album.
⇩ Mixing the album with Tony Maserati and producer Matt Rowe.

⇧ A fan with me at my last Chapters concert in Toronto.
⇩ Heading to a Dodgers game in LA on a day off.

↘ Performing at a big gala charity event.

⇧ A photo taken of my video shoot.

⇦ The big display at Chapters bookstores on release day!

⤢ Nowack and I at the press conference on release day.

⇩ Rehearsing to perform for a political campaign.

⇧ Press clippings.

⇨ The official single review in *Billboard* magazine.

⬂ Conducting a radio interview to promote "Cars."

⇩ I was on the front page of two national newspapers in the same week.

Billboard

SPOTLIGHTS — Billboard Singles Rev

NAOMI STRIEMER - CARS

Producer(s): Narada Michael Walden
Writer(s): N. Striemer
Publisher(s): S Records
Genre: POP
Label/Catalog Number: S Records
Source: Billboard Magazine
Originally Reviewed: September 23, 2006

Remember the first time you heard Whitney, Mariah or Celine and recognized a star was born? Naomi Striemer will—must—propel her foray at AC and become the commanding diva of the decade. Canadian beauty possesses so many novel traits—exalting vocals, distinctive phrasing, masterful songwriting—that 10 notes into heartbreaking first single "Cars," stares will aim toward speakers. Initially signed to an ultimately botched deal with Epic, she is now driving mission of entrepreneur Steven Nowack, who is persuading on a grass-roots level that Striemer is inevitable. Grammy Award-winning contributors Carlos Santana (guitar) and Narada Michael Walden are convinced. The year's most promising melodic debut, a standing ovation of an endorsement. —Chuck Taylor

S RECORDS

⇧ With Carlos Santana backstage at one of his concerts in Maryland where he told me I would be the "light of music."

⬈ Backstage with Steven Tyler at one of Aerosmith's concerts in Los Angeles.

⬇ We were shooting the music video for "Cars" in San Fransisco—with Carlos Santana and Narada Michael Walden.

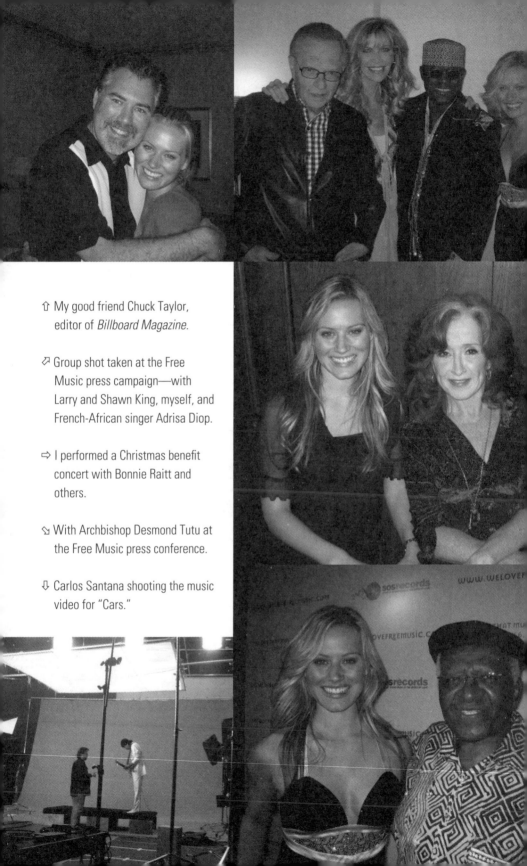

⇧ My good friend Chuck Taylor, editor of *Billboard Magazine*.

⇗ Group shot taken at the Free Music press campaign—with Larry and Shawn King, myself, and French-African singer Adrisa Diop.

⇨ I performed a Christmas benefit concert with Bonnie Raitt and others.

⇘ With Archbishop Desmond Tutu at the Free Music press conference.

⇩ Carlos Santana shooting the music video for "Cars."

⇧ A post-Grammy's recording session.

⇦ Meeting two of the artists I grew up listening to at a charity event where I performed. Rain (Our Lady Peace) and his wife, singer Chantal Kreviazuk—with myself and Nowack.

⇦ Meeting Mario Winans and his mom Vicki Winans in the studio in Detroit.

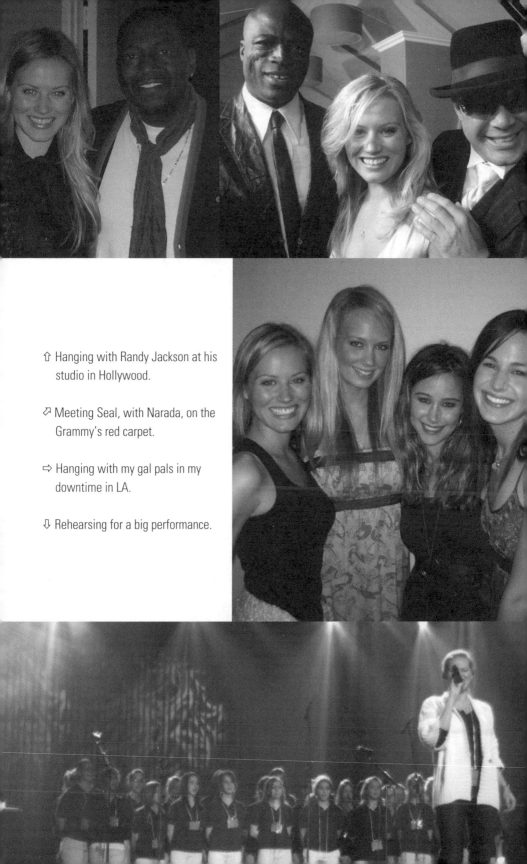

⇧ Hanging with Randy Jackson at his studio in Hollywood.

⬀ Meeting Seal, with Narada, on the Grammy's red carpet.

⇨ Hanging with my gal pals in my downtime in LA.

⇩ Rehearsing for a big performance.

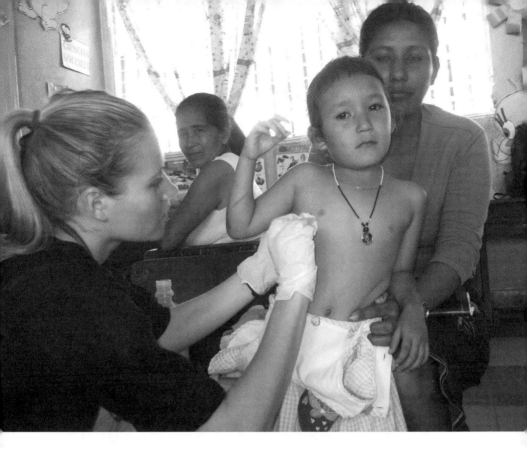

⇧ Bandaging a wound on my mission trip in Honduras.
⇩ Spending time with my parents at a charity event where I performed.

⇧ Meeting Shawn Boonstra after his closing meeting.
⇩ The night I met my husband Jordan (on the right).